The Ten Modules

Equipping You to Mobilize

The Ten Modules

The Ten Modules

The Traveling Team Press (PO Box 567, Conway, AR 72033) functions only as book publisher. As such, the ultimate design, content, editorial accuracy, and views expressed or implied in this work are those of the author.

Unless noted otherwise, all Scriptures quotations are taken from The Holy Bible, English Standard Version® (ESV®), Copyright © 2001 by Crossway, a publishing ministry of Good News Publishers. All rights reserved. ESV® Text Edition: 2016, Italics, bold, or underlined in the biblical text are added by the author for emphasis.

ISBN: 978-0-692-05671-4

The Ten Modules

Table of Contents

Introduction...6

Module 1...10
Understanding the Importance of Mobilization

Module 2...16
How to Develop World Vision

Module 3...42
How to Share the Biblical Basis of Missions

Module 4...54
How to Guide Others in the Habits of a World
Christian

Module 5...72
How to Implement Missions Into Your Ministry

Module 6...82
How to Cultivate World Prayer

Module 7...98
How to Handle Excuses

Module 8...122
How to Mobilize Your Church

Module 9...132
How to Choose the Right Mission Agency

Module 10...140
How to Raise Support

The Ten Modules

Introduction

    Mobilization, the hidden secret of world missions! Behind every missionary, whether short or long term, is a mobilizer. The mobilizer may have been a book, a dynamic speaker, the example and inspiration of a missionary of old, the scrapbook of a friend who'd gone or a mother who had faithfully prayed. Think about your own life. The fact that you are holding this little book gives testimony to the long chain of events that led you to be where you are. Your chain is much different than mine, but we were led through a process of being awakened to the grand pursuit of the world-wide worship of God! What could be a grander purpose than to "serve Him shoulder to shoulder" (Zeph. 3:9) in accomplishing His desire and the deserved reward of His sufferings? God is in the business of rallying laborers to work His fields and we praise Him for allowing our humble participation! Because the overwhelming evidence of Scripture points to God's ultimate end: the presence of "every tribe, tongue and nation, standing before the throne and in front of the Lamb," I'm convinced that there is no select elitist group of people chosen for the task. It is the responsibility of all Christians to take an active part in this Harvest! That is why I want to call all Christians to be World Christians and all World Christians to be Mobilizers!

The Traveling Team has given the same challenge to thousands of students as they have traveled to campuses across the nation. The creation of these 10 Modules is the direct result of our observations and study of the current state of mobilization among students. We have seen, in general, a heart and desire to mobilize, but an inability to move forward due to lack of knowledge. The American Heritage College Dictionary defines a module as "a standard or unit of measurement". The idea behind these modules is for the reader to be able to approach mobilization with a clear idea of how it should take place. They are not meant to be read straight through, but rather, each chapter is written in a stand-alone fashion, to be read as needed. It is our sincerest hope that these modules serve to raise up laborers from the campus to the world.

The Ten Modules

Module 1

Understanding the Importance of Mobilization

George Gallup projected 100,000 U.S. churches would close their doors between 1992-2002; not because of low funds or programs, but lack of vision. Proverbs 29:18 reaffirms this: "Where there is no vision, the people perish." Cad Dudley, Christian leader and missions enthusiast, spoke of the need to be strategic: "Congregations that intentionally affect their times have a sense of purpose and a plan; they have a vision of what God is calling them to be and to do. The person who articulates the appropriate vision for the church is both the cause and result of a mobilized church; both the church and the leaders are mutually empowered in the process."

Sadly though, it has been estimated that the time between the moment someone first gains a World Christian conviction and the time that person finally ends up working with an unreached people group is, on average, seven years. If realistic evaluation and practical World Christian discipleship are not incorporated into people's lives during these seven years they usually lose their passion and vision for the world. This is why the late Donald McGavern, founder of Fuller School of World Missions, said in his book, *A Giant Step*, "Let us furiously organize frontier mission societies in every congregation of every denomination." He was trying to tell us of the absolute necessity of people banding together to create, maintain, and follow through on their missions vision; and within the Body of Christ, the mobilizer is the one who helps orchestrate it all.

Dr. Ralph Winter, founder of the U.S. Center for World Missions comments: "Here is a tragic fact: Only about one out of a hundred 'missionary decisions' results in actual career mission service. Why? First, because few parents, pastors and friends really encourage anyone to follow through on that kind of a decision. But what if that number could double to two out of a hundred? The effect would be explosive!" No less than 100,000 sincere, envisioned people write each year to one or another of the various mission agencies in this country asking for information about possible service under that agency. The estimate is that less than 1,000 of those will ever make it to the field. Why? There is no one to nurture, guide and equip them to complete the process. In other words, the workers are plentiful, but the mobilizers are few!

A mobilizer in simplest terms is one who multiplies, disciples or mentors in missions. Phil Parshall, missionary, author and mobilizer, said it this way, "Someone must sound the rallying call. Those who desire to see others trained, prepared and released to ministry are known as mobilizers. Mobilizers stir other Christians to active concern for reaching the world. They coordinate efforts between senders, the local churches, sending agencies and missionaries on the field. Mobilizers are essential. To understand the role of mobilizers, think of World War II as a parallel. Only 10% of the American population went to the war. Of those, only 1% were actually on the firing lines. However, for them to be successful in their mission, the entire country had to be mobilized!"

What is mobilization, you ask? Wesley Tullis, formerly a Director of Prayer Mobilization for YWAM states: "Essentially mobilization refers to any process by which God's people are awakened and kept moving and growing until they find their place for strategic involvement in the task of completing world evangelization. Mobilizers are those who channel key resources, training and vision for world evangelization to the Body of Christ. It has been said, that to improperly appreciate and support the role of the mobilizer is to seriously hinder the functions of the goer, sender, and welcomer."

Dr. Winter believes that "the greatest mobilization effort in history is now gaining momentum, moving ahead with a quickening pace, and with more and more goals that are concrete, measurable and feasible." How can we participate? What are the critical components to get the job done? Winter claims, "The number one priority is for more mission mobilizers. Why do I say this? Because I believe there must be at least 40,000 younger adults who have in the past few years made a missionary decision, but who will never make it to the field - due to ignorance, indifference, baby boomer detachment, school debts, etc."

Standing before a crowd of college students, Dr. Winter challenged them, saying, "Suppose I had a thousand college seniors in front of me who asked me where they ought to go to make a maximum contribution to Christ's global cause. What would I tell them? I would tell them to stay home and mobilize. All of them." How in the world can this former missionary say this with a straight face - trying to talk people into not becoming missionaries? Because the need to sound the alarm is so great. Wouldn't it be strategic to awaken one hundred sleeping firemen rather than to throw your own little bucket of water on the huge fire yourself? Some will go as pioneer missionaries. Still others will be able to stay back from the field and assist this entire U.S. mobilization process to succeed.

When churches get involved in sending missionaries out – they want them to hold "important roles". They use words like "overseas" as if an ocean makes a difference, or "foreign field" – as if it needs to be far away, and "frontlines" – as if support personnel are not essential. There must be people who will stir the troops here declaring, "This is what is left to be done." Without them, we lose sight of the big picture and have no idea how to prioritize mission efforts. To stay and mobilize requires real faith and vision. In other words, anyone can count the seeds in an apple. But who can count the apples in just one seed?

Greg Parsons, Executive Director of the U.S. Center for World Missions, shares these innovative thoughts: "Missions mobilization is a strategic new category that churches are increasingly recognizing as key to their global outreach. It may not be in your church's missions policy.... yet, but it is becoming more and more understood by alert missions thinkers and strategizers. We are familiar with church planters, evangelists, student workers, theological educators, etc. But this new, growing category may be the most important of all... the role of the missions mobilizer. It's really not new, though, mobilization has always happened! Every missionary, whether he calls it by its name or not, has been mobilized. Churches are now realizing that if you don't have people who work at spreading vision here, you won't have people who go to "the field".

For a long time it has been ingrained into the minds of church-goers and into church culture that to arrive spiritually is to be a missionary. Well, if the Church is going to succeed in her mission, we must begin to recognize and confidently live out the different roles God has set in place in order for us to move forward. We are a body whose parts have many functions. In the end, we work toward one ultimate goal – the redemption of all nations. May we not exalt one function over another. And may we never underestimate the importance of those whose missions vision leads them to stay behind and mobilize others to the nations.

Module 2

How to Develop World Vision

Chris is a senior at the University of Tennessee and has been a Christian since he was ten years old. Coming to college has presented some tough decisions about whether or not he was going to continue to walk with God or go after the things of the world. He has chosen wisely. He has been involved in his campus ministry group over the past 3 years and something has recently happened in his own life that has really shaken him up. Chris just spent the summer in Morocco reaching out to the Muslim culture and is

16

realizing just how much that trip has changed his outlook on life. On campus he sees internationals in a different light. The things that formerly held great priority have taken a back seat. His desire to study God's word and live a holy life is at an all time high, he sees the world and word with a new perspective and he comes to the startling conclusion that the majority of the Christians on campus don't really care. What would you do?

At times it can be very frustrating when the things that people should care about are neglected. Proverbs 29:18 talks about the truth that where there is no vision the people perish. And isn't that so true? Without a vision of greater things the only thing that is important to us is ourselves! The Christian life begins to revolve around us and we lose sight of the bigger picture. It then becomes very easy to forget the fact that God intends to use His children to bring glory to His name among the nations. And most Christians have never heard that the Christian life isn't about them. No one has ever challenged them to give their life to something more than graduating early, settling down with a picket fence and the American dream. That is where you come in.

At some point in Chris's life somebody taught him the importance of world vision. Now he, in turn, is responsible to pass on the same vision. He will need some tools, some resources. Realizing that many students can identify with Chris, we have developed a simple tool to help you cast vision into the lives of other students who may not be the slightest bit interested in missions. The key is to show them their need for growth so that in turn they will be teachable to the things you can offer them. You must show them that there is more to the Christian life than what they may see.

The World Vision Illustration

The World Vision Illustration is a tool designed for you to enable others to see their need for growth in the area of becoming a World Christian and their ability to practically get there. It is designed to work best in a casual one-on-one setting or with a small group where for about 20-30 minutes you explain a simple illustration. The hopeful goal is that once the student sees his or her need to grow the opportunity will arise for you personally to train them further.

Read through this, practice it and start taking a few people through it to see how far they will let you take them. Maybe after your initial time with them you will be able to start meeting with them and educating and equipping them to see their part in God's Great Commission.

Step 1 : Christian & World Christian

Write "World Vision Illustration" at the top, center of a piece of paper in the landscape position (horizontal). Then draw two stick figures. The stick figure on the top left of the page will be labeled "Christian" while the other figure on the top center will be labeled "Global Christian."

Ask them "What do you think the difference is between the Christian and the Global Christian?"

Once these two stick figures have been drawn take some time to describe the similarities and differences between the two. For example, for similarities, say that "both are believers of Jesus, both are saved, both read their Bible, etc." However, for differences, say that "the World Christian is going to have a different perspective in 3 specific areas: God's Word, God's World, and God's Work."

Either the Typical Christian has never heard of these or just does not care about them. List them under Global Christian as you walk them through it. After each aspect you will notice there is a series of questions to ask to bring to light where the student is. As you are exploring each, feel free to go as deep as you would like.

Step 2: God's Word, World, and Work

The goal of this section is for the student to see that a Christian is not more or less holy than a Global Christian. A Global Christian simply has a different perspective on these 3 areas.

Write "God's Word" directly below the World Christian figure, then leaving about an inch of space write "God's World" and then "God's Work" about an inch below that (see below).

Steps 3, 4 and 5 have the majority of the content within the illustration. Remember, if you are talking with a very interested student, there is always the opportunity to walk through more content outside of this specific illustration.

God's Word:

Ask, "Do you know any verses regarding God's heart for the world?" Try to press them to keep giving you verses especially after they have used the usual ones. After their list, walk them through the verses below and help them see God's heart for the world from Genesis to Revelation.

The goal of this step is allowing the student to see that the convictions that a World Christian has comes from a Biblical conviction of God's heart for the World throughout scripture.

It may be helpful to point out that these verses are spread throughout Scripture. This will help reiterate the idea that God's heart for all nations is a major theme through the whole Bible. Explain to them that these verses walk through the introduction to God's mission, the plot and the conclusion. For a more thorough list of scriptures, take a look at Module 3.

Possible Verses to Explore:

> *Genesis 1:28, 9:1, 11:1-8, 12:1-4, 26:4, 28:14; Deut. 4:5-6; Joshua 2:9-10; 1 Kings 4:34; Matthew 24:14; Mark 16:15; Acts 1:8; Revelation 5:9*

To transition to the next step say, "if God has a heart for the world all throughout the bible, then we should know what the world looks like."

God's World:

The goal of this step is allowing the student to see that a World Christian will look at the World differently, if they have the biblical conviction that God has a heart for the world.

Draw a large rectangle to the right of God's World and have the student label the rectangle "10/40 window"

Ask, "Are you familiar with the 10/40 window?" If the student isn't familiar that's okay because that's what this time is for! Describe to the student that the 10/40 window stretches from 10 degrees north latitude (above the equator) to 40 degrees north latitude. The box stretches from West Africa, through the Middle East, India, Southeast Asia, China and Japan. Try to point out a few statistics about the 10/40 window to drive home the incredible urgency that this area of the world has for the gospel.

In the 10/40 window there are:

- 5 Billion People Total.

- 3 Billion Unreached People

- 97% of the Unreached People of the World

- Only 4% of Long-term, Cross Cultural Workers

(for more information on the 10/40 Window, unreached peoples, and the task remaining visit www.thetravelingteam.org/stats)

Write out the following two statistics inside the box: "97% of Unreached" on the top and "4% of Workers" on the bottom. These two statistics are two of the most striking when placed together.

Optional: World Religions

Ask, "Do you know the basic world religions?" Walk them through each of the major religions of the world using the acronym T.H.U.M.B.

T= Tribal: Found in places like Irian Jaya and Papua New Guinea. Tribal people fear spirits and are animistic in religion. There are about 3,000 Tribal groups with no access to the gospel.

H= Hinduism: Found mostly in India and Nepal. There are more worshipped deities acknowledged by Hinduism than there are people in the United States. There are about 900 million Hindus.

U= Unreligious: This category includes all of those people who have no religion. It is primarily made up of the 1.3 billion living in China. The Chinese follow atheism, Taoism, Confucianism, and other Chinese philosophies. They mainly believe that there is no God and they exalt these philosophies whose end goal is humanism.

M= Muslim: Found in North Africa and the Middle East. They believe you must adhere to the 5 pillars of Islam in order to be a good Muslim and attain heaven (pray, fast, give, say the creed, take trip to Mecca). There are about 1.2 billion Muslims. While

Indonesia has the largest Muslim population of any country, Islam spreads all the way from western North Africa to Pakistan.

B= Buddhism: Found in East Asia especially in Laos, Vietnam, and Japan. They believe there is no soul and no god. The ultimate aspiration of man is to rid himself of his desire and therefore relieve suffering. This is accomplished by meditation and multiple reincarnations. There are about 600 million Buddhists.

After you have walked them through this it is good to refer back to the Typical Christian and ask them what this person thinks about the THUMB. Compare the perspective of the Typical Christian with the perspective of the Global Christian.

Questions to ask about God's World:

Ask, "Why do you think that only 4% of workers decide to go there?" They will typically give answers revolving around language, culture, safety and access to Americans. Affirm them in their answers telling them that it could be difficult and maybe even dangerous. Then ask, "Why do you think those 4% of workers decided to go anyway?" They will typically give answers revolving around a call. Affirm the student in that, but point back up to the God's Word section and describe that we are all called to play a part. End with saying, these 4% saw the need and saw that God was worth whatever difficulties they would face. To transition to the next step say, "If this is what God's Word says and this is what the world looks like, then what do we do about it? Let's talk about God's Work"

God's Work:

The goal of this section is for the student to walk away with practical steps when it comes to living out the World Christian lifestyle. Show them that the Global Christian is a believer who is actively involved in God's work no matter where they are geographically.

28

Help explain the various habits of a Global Christian. To the right of "God's Work" write out "GO" and then below that write "SEND". Next to "GO" write "HERE" and "THERE". Next to "SEND" write "PRAY" and "GIVE"

There are a lot of ways to challenge students when it comes to these 4 habits of being a World Christian. We have found it to be a best practice to explain each of the habits in simple terms and then give one or two practical next steps within that habit.

GO HERE — (also known as "welcoming") as a Global Christian we should notice that the nations are right here in our backyard! We have people from the 10/40 window sitting next to us in classes, at coffee shops or at work. God has brought unreached people to the U.S. so that we can befriend them and share the good news with them! It would be criminal for an unreached student to come to the U.S. to never hear the gospel and then go back to their closed country where they will never hear to gospel again. Challenge the student to make one more friend.

GO THERE — as a Global Christian we should know that the unreached will not be reached unless people actually go to them to take the good news. Challenge the student to get connected with an organization or mission agency that could send them on a summer trip to get face to face with the unreached. (Have them fill out a form at www.missionagency.org if they are without their own connections)

SEND by PRAYING — as a Global Christian we should desire to pray for the things that God's heart is for. Jesus says in Luke 10:2 to "pray earnestly to the Lord of the harvest to send out workers into his harvest." Challenge the student to set an alarm for 10:02 every day to pray for workers. Also challenge the student to download the "JP Unreached" app on their phone.

SEND by GIVING — as a Global Christian we should desire to give financially to those who are going and playing a part in the Great Commission. Challenge the student that if they do not begin a habit of sacrificial giving now when they don't have money, then it will not get any easier for them when they do start to make money. In every season of life there will always be excuses. Challenge the student to give up something once or twice a week in order to set that money aside for works. An $8 meal at a restaurant given up weekly equals up to about $40/month to give.

For more information on how to GO and SEND visit www.thetravelingteam.org/go-send

30

To transition to the next step say, "We have seen that the Global Christian understands God's Word, God's World, and God's Work. Let's jump back up to the Christian."

Step 3 : Growth as a Global Christian

The goal of this section is for the student to take an inward look at themselves to see the room they have to grow as a World Christian. Draw a horizontal line between the two stick men and ask them to place themselves on the line according to where they think they are in the process of becoming a Global Christian. At this point the best thing to do is to *hand them the pen and let them mark on the line.*

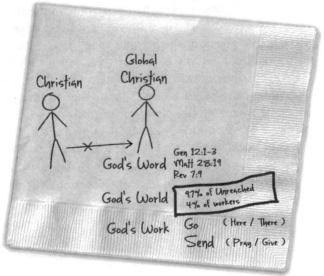

This is the key to your entire time and this will help them see their need to grow more than anything else. Explain to the student that the line is a growth spectrum that is evaluating where the student thinks they are in becoming a Global Christian. To the far left this line represents someone who doesn't know anything about God's Word, God's World, and God's Work. To the far right this line represents someone who is living out God's Word, God's World, and God's Work on a daily basis.

Give time to the student to think about this a put a mark on the line where they are on the growth spectrum.

Explain to the student that everyone has room to grow when it comes to being a World Christian and nobody wakes up as a World Christian. It is a life long process of aligning our hearts with God's heart for the world. Encourage them to take steps by praying, giving, welcoming and going to the unreached.

Ask them what it would take for them to become a Global Christian? What would their life look like? How would this change the way they live life right now? Explain to them that God wants them to become a Global Christian and that, most importantly, you would like to help them get there.

Step 4: Tools for Growth:

The bottom line is to grow in a heart for the world and they will need resources in order to do that. The next thing to do is to walk them through very practical steps as to how they can move closer to being a Global Christian. Here is a list of some basics to start them with. Feel free to add new ones.

- **Mission Trips-** Share with them the importance of their summer and how they choose to spend it. Link them into the various agencies that you know of, and give them examples of the trips they offer. Be sure to cast vision for the potential of short-term trips.

- **Websites-** Explain to them the major websites that will help them move towards this goal by providing resources like articles, world news and educational statistics for them. Some examples are thetravelingteam.org, calebproject.org, urbana.org (See Appendix D for more information)

- **Books-** Help them to see the value of building a missions library while they are in college. Give them examples of books that have impacted your life and tell them how they can buy those books. (For more information on great books see Appendix D)

- **Beginners Guide to Global Christianity-** On The Traveling Team website thetravelingteam.org/beginners-guide-to-global-impact there are lessons that they can print off or work through on-line that explain the basics in becoming a Global Christian.

- **Reaching out to Internationals-** Cast vision for them to begin to notice the amount of internationals that are in the community and on the campus. Help them with some practical steps of reaching out to them (i.e. have them over, take them out for a meal, help them with their English, give them a ride somewhere, etc.).

- **Prayer-** Show them the way to bring God's heart for the world to their prayer time. Help them to utilize vital resources such as: Operation World, People Group Profiles, a World Map, etc.

Let them know that you are excited about their journey in becoming a Global Christian and that you would love for them to join with you as you both grow in God's heart for the world.

To transition to the next step say, "A Christian doesn't become a World Christian all on their own. There is a third person who enables this to happen, and that's the Mobilizer."

Step 5: The Power of a Mobilizer

If the student you are meeting with seems hungry to learn and is teachable, you might want to continue to cast vision for them as a Campus Mobilizer. What we mean by Campus Mobilizer is someone who has taken personal responsibility to see other students catch a vision for the world. A Campus Mobilizer has learned the skills needed to help students gain a heart for the world.

Transition to their specific potential and how you would like to see them impart vision to others as a college student.

Example: "I am excited about your journey in learning all that God has for you in this area. You know, I think that once you grow in these three areas that you will have a lot to offer these students who have not been exposed to the things that you have. Can I ask you to consider something else...I would like for you to consider becoming a Campus Mobilizer. What this means is that not only are you going to grow in these areas, but that you will take personal responsibility for the Christian students on this campus and help them grow as well."

Draw the third stick man past the Global Christian and label him Campus Mobilizer.

Campus Mobilizer

Ask them what they think the difference between a Global Christian and a Campus Mobilizer is.

The goal of this step is for the student to see that mobilization is a needed step in seeing the Great Commission fulfilled and that they can start mobilizing people today.

Show them that the Global Christian is focused on learning the three areas, but a Campus Mobilizer can actually teach a person who is a Christian to become a Global Christian.

Brief them on what a Campus Mobilizer's role would be on campus: one who is thinking through creative ways to impart missions vision to other Christian students. They are strategizing, planning and praying through the best ways to carry this out. Whether in small group Bible studies or within the large group meetings they are trying to keep God's heart for the world in front of others.

Explain to them their potential to impact the campus. Paint a picture of what it might look like to see students launched out from your campus to the world.

Explain that a Christian doesn't become a World Christian all on their own. Draw an arched line from the Mobilizer across the top of the page to the Christian. Explain that a Mobilizer helps the Christian become a Global Christian. The Mobilizer helps that Christian understand God's Word, God's World, and God's Work.

Celebrate the fact that when a Christian becomes a Global Christian that is plus one (+1) for the team! That's one more person who see's the theme throughout God's Word, who sees the need in the world, and desires to go and send.

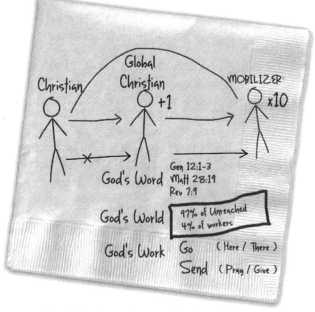

Explain that when we look at the needs of the world and the work before us, we need more than simply addition, we need MULTIPLICATION! Cast vision to the student telling them that we don't only want them to become a Global Christian, but we also want them to become a Mobilizer. It's one of the actions that a Global Christian should prioritize.

Explain that when a World Christian also becomes a Mobilizer that is not just plus one (+1) but this becomes a multiplication effect of times ten (x10), times twenty (x20), and more! This is a process that will allow a World Christian movement to happen.

The final challenge is to have the student write the name of two people in their lives that they could share this World Vision Illustration with.

After walking a student through the World Vision Illustration, help them process through individual next steps. As you process through sharing the World Vision Illustration with students, here are some helpful tips:

- Share your own personal stories of welcoming internationals, ways that you've given or prayed.

- For resources go to *www.thetravelingteam.org*.

- For connection to go overseas go to *www.missionagency.org*.

Final Thoughts:

Every Christian should be a World Christian. Unfortunately, most of us would never arrive at that conclusion without someone else's explanation. Therefore, it must be true that every Global Christian should be a Mobilizer. Students, more than any other group of people, are in a position to do this.

The Ten Modules

Module 3

How to Share the Biblical Basis of Missions

Scott grew up in a good Christian home with godly, committed parents. He was in church every Sunday morning and night and was raised with an understanding of the principles of God. He went to a Christian high school where he was awarded student of the year and headed off to college to pursue baseball on full scholarship. At college Scott plugged into a

42

good church, led worship and tried to be a witness on his baseball team. Scott had a good life planned out: try to make it into professional baseball, continue his walk with God, and if baseball fails, become a worship leader at a mega-church. Then one Tuesday afternoon Scott's life took a dramatic turn. A friend of his sat him down and started probing him about his heart for the world. Scott gave him the good Christian answer and said that he loved the world, but that God had called him here to play baseball. As his friend started pressing a little more and asking for missions verses and his knowledge of the world, Scott had to plead ignorance and admitted that he could not name but one missions verse. His friend went to work.

Starting with Genesis, Scott spent the next 30 minutes being walked through God's heart for the world. Through the life of Abraham, Isaac and Jacob, it began to click for Scott that he really was unaware of God's priority to redeem all peoples. Finally, the story culminated when he read Rev. 5:9 and saw the story's conclusion: what God had promised Abraham about blessing all nations is fulfilled in Revelation. Scott was floored. How could he have been a Christian practically his whole life and never have heard the missions theme of scripture? After more learning and praying Scott decided to quit baseball, finish college, and use his music talent to reach the unreached tribal people in Papua New Guinea.

What if you spent some time learning how to help people like Scott on your campus gain a heart for the world? What if you cultivated the ability to walk people through God's mission vision from His Word? That is where this module comes in. Here is a basic outline you can use for showing people God's mission vision in a small group or one-on-one setting.

As you sit down with your group or individual, begin by challenging them to look at the Bible as one book and show them that you can divide the Bible into three parts: *An Introduction:* Genesis 1-11, *a Plot:* from Genesis 12 all the way to the book of Jude, and a *Conclusion:* Revelation.

Begin by looking at the Introduction. Read Genesis 1:28 "God blessed them and said to them, "Be fruitful and multiply; fill the earth..." Help them to see that God, from the beginning, desired man to populate the earth both physically and spiritually. God knew that as Adam and Eve "filled the earth" with their physical descendants, they would be filling the earth with worshippers of God as they passed on their spiritual heritage. Help them picture the world full of worshippers as God intended. Explain that because of the fall of man in Genesis 3:1-8, every thought of man was evil by Genesis 6:5. Consequently, God flooded the earth and started over with one family.

Read Genesis 9:1 "Then God blessed Noah and his sons saying to them, "Be fruitful and multiply and fill the earth." Observe that God repeats His command to fill the earth. The crucial question to have in mind while reading chapters 10-11 is, "Does God get it? Will He get the world populated?" God has commanded it twice; it must be important to Him.

Read Genesis 11: 1-8 "Now the whole world had one language and a common speech. As men moved eastward, they found a plain in Shinar and settled there...Then they said, 'Come, let us build ourselves a city, with a tower that reaches to the heavens, so that we may make a name for ourselves and not be scattered over the face of the whole earth. Come, let us go down and confuse their language so they will not understand each other.' So the Lord scattered them from there over all the earth, and they stopped building the city."

Ask them, "Why didn't the people scatter? What was their desire? How did God respond?" This is an extremely important chapter in Scripture, and it will be vital that you pass on its significance to your group or individual. It is so important because for the first time we see the diversity of man. Up until now they have been one communal whole. Since man did not fulfill the command to populate the earth and spread out, God took it upon Himself to make sure they obeyed by creating the various language groups and scattering them all over the earth. Sum up the introduction by explaining what the world looked like at this point in history with man spread out all over the earth speaking many different languages.

Transition to the plot. Help them to see that God's plan of receiving worship from all peoples on earth had not changed. In fact, the rest of scripture is an unfolding of this plan and how He will accomplish it. In this next passage we see the method God chose to launch His plan and the method He chooses today: people.

Read Genesis 12:1-4 "The Lord had said to Abram, 'Leave your country, your people and your father's household and go to the land I will show you...I will bless you...and all peoples on earth will be blessed through you.' "So Abram left, as the Lord had told him."

It's important that you point out that God chose Abram from all the nations on the earth (those scattered at Babel) so that through him God might reach the world. Abram's obedience meant that he would have to leave his own country and go to the new land that God would show him. Here are some questions to ask: What would you have done if you were Abram? Would you have left? Why or why not?

Explain that God's desire to reach all peoples

does not stop with Abraham, but the rest of the plot (Genesis 12-Jude) is the story of God using people for the purpose of reaching the world. Talk through these different passages starting with Abraham's descendants:

Abrahams' son Isaac: Genesis 26:4 "I will make your descendants as numerous as the stars in the sky and will give them all these lands, and through your offspring all nations on earth will be blessed."

Isaac's son Jacob: Genesis 28:14 "Your descendants will be like the dust of the earth, and you will spread out to the west and to the east, to the north and to the south. All peoples on earth will be blessed through you and your offspring"

Walk them through the rest of the Old Testament observing how God would do things in accordance with His desire for the nations to come to know Him. Here are some examples you could use:

The 10 Commandments: Ever wonder why God gave us the Ten Commandments? The obvious answer is so that His children could obey Him, but there is more. As we read what Moses says about the commandments we see God's vision for all peoples to know Him. Ultimately, His plan was to have a people so set apart that as the nations looked on they couldn't help but give glory to God.

Deuteronomy 4:5-6 "See, I have taught these decrees and laws as the Lord my God has commanded me. Observe them carefully, for this will show your wisdom and understanding to the nations, who will hear about all these decrees and say, 'Surely this great nation is a wise and understanding people.'"

Parting the Red Sea: God delivered His people from the bondage of the mighty Egyptian empire. News of such a catastrophic event was sure to travel fast! The Israelites not only escaped from Egypt, but also parted the Red Sea! Look at the glory God gets from just one of the surrounding nations who heard about this miracle.

Joshua 2:9-10 "I (Rahab) know that the Lord has given this land to you and that a great fear of you has fallen on us...we have heard how the Lord dried up the water of the Red Sea for you when you came out of Egypt..."

Solomon and his wisdom: God gave King Solomon a great gift; He made the king wiser than any other man on earth. Why did God give Solomon this wisdom? Was it because He loved him? Was it because he needed it to be king? Was it because He wanted to bless him? These are all good answers, but look at it from a different perspective. Look at what happened when the nations heard this about the wisdom God had given Solomon.

1 Kings 4:34 "The whole world sought audience with Solomon to hear the wisdom God had put in his heart."

Shadrach, Meshach and Abednego: King Nebuchadnezzar was a wicked king who was greedy for glory. He was so greedy for it that when he constructed a huge golden idol and commanded everyone to bow to it, he decided that anyone who defied him would be burned to death in a furnace. Three men would not bow to the king's statue because of their devotion to God. Consequently, they were thrown into the furnace, but God miraculously saved them. Look at King Nebuchadnezzar's response when he witnessed this act. The story becomes yet another example of God's desire to be worshipped in all the earth.

Daniel 3:29: "Therefore, I (Nebuchadnezzar) decree that the people of any nation or language who say anything against the God of Shadrach, Meshach and Abednego be cut into pieces... for no other God can save in this way."

Daniel in the lions' den: Daniel was exiled in a land not his own under the authority of a pagan king. Yet he was fully devoted to serving God. And it would cost him. King Darius' men had him thrown into a den of lions to be eaten alive and done away with. Yet God in His grace extended His arm of protection to Daniel, and he was unharmed. As the king witnesses this act, we see once again God's name being made known throughout all the earth.

Daniel 6:25-26 "Then King Darius wrote to all the peoples, nations, and men of every language who were living in all the land... I (Darius) issue a decree that in every part of my kingdom people must fear and reverence the God of Daniel..."

For further verses, see Psalm 33:13-14, 67:1-7, 86:9-10, 96:3; Isaiah 11:9-10, 49:6, 52:10, 61:11; Jonah 4:11, Habakkuk 1:5, Zephaniah 2:11, Haggai 2:7, Zechariah 8:20-23, Malachi 1:11.

As you transition to the New Testament show them that the plot continues. As Christ—God in flesh—enters the scene, help them identify His ministry pattern of reaching out to all nations. Here are a few examples:

Clearing the temple: Mark 11:15-17, "On reaching Jerusalem, Jesus entered the temple area designated for the Gentiles to worship and He found people buying and selling there. As He drove them out saying 'Is it not written; "My house will be called a house of prayer for all nations?"'

The sign of Jesus' return: Matthew 24:14, "And this gospel of the kingdom will be preached in the whole world as a testimony to all nations, and then the end will come."

Jesus' ministry: Luke 4:42-43, "...they tried to keep him from leaving them, but He said, 'I must preach the good news of the kingdom of God to the other towns also, because that is why I was sent.'"

Jesus' mandate to His followers: Mark 16:15, "Go into all the world and preach the good news to all creation."

Explain that the book of Acts and the Epistles are a testimony of the account of the gospel spreading outward. It begins with Jesus echoing what He taught the disciples for the past 3 years and ends with letters to the churches that had just been planted by missionaries.

Acts 1:8, "But you will receive power when the Holy Spirit comes on you; and you will be my witnesses in Jerusalem, and in all Judea and Samaria, and to the ends of the earth."

As soon as the church experiences persecution, they scatter (Acts 8:1), and the Lord adds great numbers to their missionary force. *Acts 9:15 "...Go! This man (Paul) is my chosen instrument to carry my name before the Gentiles..."*

Here's the recap: the introduction in Genesis 1-11, the plot throughout Genesis 12-Jude, and now the conclusion:

Revelation 7:9, "After this I looked and there before me was a great multitude that no one could count, from every nation, tribe, people, and language, standing before the throne and in front of the Lamb..."

It is important that you connect for them that what is happening in Revelation was the very thing God started in Genesis 12 in the life of Abraham. God will do it! There will be a representative from every nation, tribe, people, and language bowing and worshipping at His feet. Heaven is multicultural. God is a missionary God and from cover to cover He is showing us His mission. Here are some good questions to conclude with:

• Do you see God's heart for the world? Would you like to continue to grow in this area? Were there any familiar stories that you had never seen from a missions perspective? Would you like to get more resources on this subject?

Help them make a list of some practical things they can do within the week to start to implement God's heart for the world into their own life. Make yourself available for questions they may have.

Final Thoughts:

No one would ever tell you that God's mission was a bad idea. In fact, just about every church would affirm its great value and importance! Yet, how many Christians know what the Bible has to say about it? How many think it is important because God thinks it is important? Disturbingly few. Without the authority of God's Word, missions will remain just a good idea. It will forever be just a suggestion holding little to no priority for the average Christian. The Biblical basis for missions is a foundational tool in the belt of every mobilizer. The above information is the reason we mobilize with confidence.

For other New Testament verses, see: *Matthew 9:35-38, 28:18-20; John 20:21, Romans 10:11-15, 15:20; Galatians 3:13-14, I Timothy 2:4-6, II Peter 3:9, I John 2:2*

Module 4

How to Guide Others in the Habits of a World Christian

My wife and I were driving on the highway doing about 80 miles per hour. All of a sudden I saw break lights ahead and a major traffic jam. As we closed in on the pile up of cars, I realized that the cause of the traffic jam was a terrible accident. The timing was horrible because just as we were able to see what was going on, they were pulling a dead body from the wreckage. It was something I will never forget. It impacted me so much that after we made it through the jam, let's just say I wasn't driving 80. I dropped down to around 60 miles per hour. I was far more cautious and attentive. Our conversation took on a whole new tone; we turned the radio off and made our way into the slow lane. There was something I noticed, though. The farther removed I got from the lights, the sirens, the bodies...the more I lightened up. Not only that, I sped up! Why? Maybe my memory is bad. Maybe I was already thinking of something else. Maybe I let the experience slip away!

This is a good parallel of a short term mission trip. Up until the day we leave, we are consumed with the world around us, trying to finish school, buying the next hit worship album and hanging out with friends. Then off we go for three weeks to Honduras and...WHAM! Reality hits. We are moved beyond imagination by the street kids, the impoverished condition, the hospitality of the people, and their openness to the gospel.

Never before have we been so confronted, so changed. We vow never to shop at the Gap again, have passionate quiet times daily and burn for our peers to know the same incredible zeal that consumes us! Soon though, and very subtly, normal-ness creeps its way back in. And before we know it, the scrapbook under our bed is the sole remains of the summer that "changed us."

Is this as good as it gets? Should we just slough this off as status quo? Ho-hum, that's just what happens? I don't think so. I believe there is a deeper issue here. I think that as long as missions remains a geographical issue, the result will be a lot of Christian American dreamers with mission trip scrapbooks. If our missionary to Honduras had made missions a heart issue, the few months after his trip would have looked a lot different. His trip would have been the fuel for his passion, not the basis for it.

Once missions moves beyond the geographical issue and becomes more of a heart issue, no matter where you are you are still actively involved in reaching all nations. So how is that achieved? By carrying out the various habits identified in a World Christian. Not only should you be involved personally, but help others around you to incorporate the habits of a World Christian.

The main habits are: Going, Praying, Sending, Welcoming, and Mobilizing

Everyone desiring to move toward God's heart for the world needs to cultivate these habits and be aware of how to live them out in daily life. As someone interested in mobilizing others, you need to be familiar with and well grounded in these. You also need to have the ability to equip students to live them out during college and in life beyond college. A good place to start with the student is by sitting down and talking through what a World Christian would look like on a college campus. Here are some questions that might help you get started:

- How would a World Christian spend their time?

- How would they spend their money?

- What kinds of conversations would they have?

- What would an average week be like?

You will probably find that the student's answers do not include a very wide range of things. Maybe they focus on one or two aspects of being a World Christian, or maybe they think only of someone who goes overseas. Your explanation of the following five habits will help missions to be a daily application for them as it should be.

Going:

This habit is most commonly associated with missions. In the past and even still today when someone thinks about missions this is the most natural association. A definition of the goer is the person physically present, laboring on the mission field. Going may mean a short-term trip or an extended amount of time. Ultimately, goers are willing to completely immerse themselves in an unfamiliar culture with the intention of furthering the gospel in that culture. They are innovative, low maintenance, steadfast, and persevere with little fellowship.

In Exodus 3:7-10 God mentions to Moses nine different times that He is concerned with the Israelites and their condition as slaves and is getting ready to bring them into the promise land. During this discourse, God has one reference to Moses. Look at Moses' reaction, "But Moses said to God, 'Who am I, that I should go to Pharaoh and bring the Israelites out of Egypt;' (Exodus 3:11). Sounds like us sometimes. Our temptation is to focus on ourselves and our insufficiency! We think there is no way God could want us involved and so many of us never enjoy the blessing of participating. Look at God's reaction; He puts the focus back on Himself in the next verse, "I will be with you" (Exodus 3:12).

Before Robert Morrison left to be the first Bible translator in China, someone asked if he really thought he could change the 2,000 year problem of idolatry in China. His response, "No I don't, but I expect God can." As you begin to challenge others to consider going on a short-term trip, it will be natural for them to look at their abilities (or inabilities) and become discouraged. It is at this point that you must remind them, "But God chose the foolish things of the world to shame the wise; God chose the weak things of the world to shame the strong. He chose the lowly things of this world and the despised things – and the things that are not – to nullify the things that are, so that no one may boast before him" (1 Corinthians 1:27-29). In light of this truth we are all overqualified!

Due to modern technology a person can be anywhere the world in less than 17 hours. What an incredible opportunity! Even if a person feels they should not go long-term, I think it is worthwhile to invest some time in a cross-cultural experience. It will be to the benefit of any Christian seeking to have a heart for the world as God does. A good place to begin cultivating this desire into a student's heart is to ask them if the Lord has laid a country or religion on their heart. If so, where do they see themselves? Help them to get information on all agencies that are currently working in related areas. This will make going a tangible, do-able thing. It will also be helpful to discuss the potential roadblocks that might distract them from carrying this out.

Praying:

If you could ask Jesus to teach you anything what would it be? Personally, I think I would want to learn how He multiplied the bread to feed the 5,000! Can you imagine? Well, in all of the scriptures we see only one time when the disciples ask Jesus to teach them something. The request, "Lord, teach us to pray." (Luke 11:1). Isn't it interesting that after knowing and living with Jesus, their desire was to pattern His prayer life? Maybe after following Him around for a few years they realized that when Jesus prayed, things happened. Listen to Christ's response: "This, then, is how you should pray: Our Father in heaven, hallowed be your name, *your kingdom come, your will be done on earth as it is in heaven...*" (Matt. 6:9-10).

Jesus was saying that when you pray, you should ask God to bring the activity of heaven down to earth. In other words, pray that what is going on up there, would go on down here. Well, what is going on in heaven? Right now in heaven all eyes are on Jesus, as a multicultural worship service is being held. Sound like your church? This is what Jesus asked his disciples to pray.

Another passage that challenges us to pray for the world is found in Matt 9:36-38: "When he saw the crowds, he had compassion on them, because they were harassed and helpless, like sheep without a shepherd. Then he said to his disciples, 'The harvest is plentiful but the workers are few. Ask the Lord of the harvest, therefore, to send out workers into his harvest field.'" Jesus saw the vastness of lost souls compared to the scarcity of the laborers and He looked to the disciples and said, "Ask" What a powerful image! Not go, or preach, or have a conference, but ask. It's hard to read this passage and not get convicted about your prayer life.

Let's evaluate our own prayer lives and see if we come to God with our desires or if we are concerned with His. Obviously, we need to pray for ourselves and yes, we need to lift up our family and friends, but God also desires that we join together and intercede on behalf of all nations and beg Him to send forth laborers into the field.

As you are implementing world prayer into your own life, help others to understand the importance of coming to Him and bearing His burdens. Hebrew 7:25 says, "Therefore He is able to save completely those who come to God through Him, because He always lives to intercede for them." If Christ is daily living to pray for those who come to know Him, I think it is worthy of my time and cultivation.

Sending:

Paul the Apostle has an interesting observation, "And how can they preach unless they are sent?" (Rom. 10:15). The unreached do not have a chance at hearing the gospel if there are not people on the home front funding and praying for those that are going. It is like asking the question, "Which is more important: the rescuer who goes down into the well to save a life or the man at the top holding the rope?" You can't have one without the other. There was a principle in Israelite warfare, "The share of the man who stayed with the supplies is to be the same as that of him who went down to the battle. All will share alike." (1 Sam. 30:24-25). Why? Because they are equally important in God's army.

In our culture we think we are entitled to live at whatever standard matches our income. Our reasoning is that since a person makes $60,000 a year they should live at $60,000. When a person gets a raise, their standard of living gets a raise too! But the World Christian should have a different mindset. Maybe when a Christian gets a raise or comes into unexpected financial gain, God intends that person to be a resource for someone else! This thinking is so contrary to our culture. Challenge the student to set an appropriate amount to live on and help him develop healthy convictions about the stewardship of giving.

Bill Stearns in his book, *Run With the Vision*, explains this point well:

"How different are World Christians from other Christians? In some ways, very little. They still spend much of their time doing day-to- day chores, filling their role in life (being a parent, spouse, friend), fulfilling the requirements of a job, fixing things around the house. They too work on character issues in their own life, study the scriptures, read Christian books, seek to be broken and humble before God. Both seek to keep the great commandment, loving God and loving others. But in other ways, they are very different. The World Christian uses his free time differently, keeping in mind a global perspective. He prays more for the nations and helps others catch the vision for God's glory throughout the world. He spends his finances wisely, freeing up more money for the global expansion of the kingdom. He always envisions how his ministry and activities can somehow result in eventually having an impact in the nations."

Living a World Christian lifestyle as a sender doesn't mean taking a vow of poverty—since poverty isn't necessarily spiritual and wealth isn't necessarily unspiritual. But being good stewards of money as we seek first the Kingdom of heaven is definitely a mark of a World Christian sender The lifestyle of a globally significant sender isn't mostly about money, it's about character.

The role of a sender is not only integral, but diverse as well. The most obvious aspect of sending is giving of one's financial resources to support a missionary. But this is certainly not the only facet of sending. A sender may work in one of or all the following specialized roles: logistics, prayer coordination, communications, research, finances, or re-entry coordinator. A specialist in logistics deals with the practical side of sending. They deal with packing the missionary's goods, travel plans, cost and acquirement of items needed on the field. The prayer coordinator can find specific prayer needs based on research, missionaries in the field, and missions societies. They are also needed to enlist others in intercessory prayer for the team and organize special prayer meetings. For prayer needs to be known, a communications specialist is enormously helpful. It is their responsibility to open lines of communication to the team so that prayer requests and equipment and other needs are known.

The role of sending is neither glamorous nor easy. The task of dealing with the day-to- day, behind the scenes tasks of mission work may even seem thankless, but it is not without reward. This is a seemingly difficult habit for college students to develop because they always feel broke! But the point is not the amount that is given. The point is that they are building a habit of sacrifice. No matter their income, help them to diligently set aside a portion to invest in missions.

Welcoming:

America hosts the largest number of

internationals of any country; the world is at our doorstep! Over 650,000 international students and scholars are studying here from 188 countries of the world. What a perfect opportunity to extend God's grace and love to the world! And you don't even have to leave. The welcomer gets his name from the idea that he welcomes those from other countries to his country.

The foreigner is close to the Lord's heart. Over forty times in the Old Testament alone we are commanded to care for the foreigner in our land:

"The alien living with you must be treated as one of your native-born. Love him as yourself, for you were aliens in Egypt. I am the Lord your God." (Lev 19:34).

"He defends the cause of the fatherless and the widow, and loves the alien, giving him food and clothing. And you are to love those who are aliens, for you yourselves were aliens in Egypt" (Deut 10:18-20).

God reminds the Israelites of their past exile in Egypt so that they will be motivated to love the foreigners, for they once were foreigners. Similarly, we should be reminded of our past, how we were foreigners to God and yet he had mercy on us.

Sadly, as available as this ministry is to college students, it is going sorely overlooked. Did you know that 80% of the internationals on your campus will never be invited into an American home? With high hopes they come to study, but soon realize that the hospitality they are used to is just as foreign to America as they are. So they live in their isolated community with fellow internationals and eventually return to their homeland. I wonder what they tell their friends about this renowned Christian nation.

Everyone can be a welcomer. All it takes is a little time, energy, and a willingness to say hello. There is no reason that Christians on campus shouldn't have 2-3 new international friends each semester. Can you imagine how the gospel would spread if that were a reality? At the college I attended, there were 80 students from Saudi Arabia who hung out in their corner of the Student Center. I can remember the first time I took two guys from my Bible study to meet and get to know them. After a few weeks of just saying hello and making ourselves available we became part of the group. We shared the gospel with about 10 of them over the next year. It's amazing to think of the hardship I would face should I go to Saudi Arabia and try to do the same thing! Yet here we have complete freedom to share with otherwise unreached people!

The need for welcoming is great. Help the student brain storm ideas to show love to the foreigners among you. A simple beginning step is to take them and initiate conversation with an international on your campus. There are tons of questions you could ask to get to know them:

- Where are you from?

- How do you like the food?

- How do you like it here?

- Is English harder than you thought?

- How it is different from your country?

- Are you finding your way around?

- Can we help you in anything?

You might choose a specific group of them to focus on. You and the students should regularly make yourselves ready to serve. Here are some suggested ways to do that:

- Run errands for them or be willing to take them on errands.

- Invite them over for holidays.

- Practice English with them.

- Invite them to Bible study.

- Invite them just to hang out with you and your friends.

The one who welcomes is willing to serve them and reach out to them in the hopes that Christ will be glorified. They will see how easy it is to get involved and soon they will be loving internationals and this strategic ministry.

Mobilizing:

A mobilizer is a normal, everyday Christian who walks with God, yet has a global perspective and stays on the home front to rouse others to action. Anyone who has a vision for the world has at one time been mobilized. Whether someone asked them to go on a short-term trip, invited them to a missions conference, took them to a Bible study on the topic or introduced them to a missionary, somehow they were recruited. And that, in a nutshell, is a mobilizer: a recruiter. Mobilizers are out looking for others to enlist in God's agenda with their entire life. Their focus is Christians who are unaware of God's global plan and they consistently seek to raise the missions awareness in creative ways whether it is in a small group or large group setting.

Like Habakkuk, they "write down the vision and make it plain on tablets so that the one who reads it may run" (Hab 2:2). A friend of mine has a saying that I have adopted. "Every Christian a World Christian and every World Christian a mobilizer."

Think about the awesome potential in that statement. Every Christian is orchestrating their life around God's heart for the world and fulfilling the Great Commission and at the same time passing on that vision to the new believers and next generation. Unbelievable!

So what exactly are the characteristics of a mobilizer? Bill Stearns lists 10:

- Needs to be able to be a servant.

- Desires to see laborers raised up to finish the task of world evangelization.

- Possibly has gifts of encouragement and exhortation.

- Is "apt to teach"; but may be more effective in recruiting others to teach.

- Speaks in front of groups without (too much) fear.

- Leads others well.

- Has a general heart for the world, possibly focusing in on one people group

- Sees the priority of waiting and mobilizing others as well as going.

69

- Is part visionary - seeing what can happen as God matches empowered believers with key opportunities of ministry

- Is part implementer - driven to see a vision become a reality.

In order to train others in mobilization, it is critical that you pass on the ability to find resources and tools. Whether it is just the right missions book or a short video, magazine, agency, prayer profile, etc. you need to be able to show others how to get it.

I can remember when I was in college gathering my own collection of tools. I labeled a manila folder "Mobilization Resources." Now it fills two filing cabinets! Part of being equipped with resources is being a networker. You will need to know what God is doing and who He is doing it with. I challenge anyone trying to cultivate their mobilization skills to help others collect and learn how to use the resources and material available in missions. As they are collecting and learning this material they are building a confidence that will enable them to teach others. The mobilizer is a key player in the process of raising up laborers. It takes a burning heart for the world and yet a willingness to stay. It has happened to every World Christian and every World Christian can do it!

Final Thoughts:

In order for missions to permeate your life at all times, on all levels, you will need to get beyond the mission trip burnout. It is not about a summer trip; it's not about 10 summer trips! It is about your life reflecting the heart of God no matter your location. God has always been about redeeming all nations and we should reflect that through going ourselves, sending others, welcoming internationals, praying for the world, and mobilizing Christians to go.

Module 5

How to Implement Missions into Your Ministry

The problem with missions is that most of our culture is exposed to it once or twice a year at best. The annual church missions conference held on Wednesday night is our only dosage! If we're lucky, we might get a Sunday night update from the youth about their trip to New Mexico that summer. I don't want to be overly cynical, but I don't think I'm too far off from the truth of the situation. And the result is inevitable —

a church full of people who are uneducated and therefore uninterested. The saddest thing a mobilizer hears is, "why haven't I ever heard this before?" Even more sad is the fact that it is one of the most often heard phrases for a mobilizer. Missions has become a super-spiritual aspiration for the Christian elite and is therefore far removed from normal Christian living.

So what is the goal of mobilization? Most of us are familiar with the ultimate goal: reaching every tongue, tribe, and nation. But how do we get there from here? As mobilizers, what is it that we want students to do? Cross an ocean? Reach out to internationals? Pray for the world? These are all great things, however, we do not want to mobilize students to a single activity. If we do, they go back to life as usual once the activity is completed. Instead, we should mobilize them to a change of perspective. What they previously thought of as super-spiritual, elite and once-a-year we want them daily to take personal responsibility for, so that no matter where they are or what they are doing, they are World Christians. When the missions conference is over, they are still actively pursuing a World Christian lifestyle.

This transition occurs over a period of time, and below is an outline of that process. The crucial thing to remember when mobilizing is that as applicable and relevant as you make your heart for the world is to the same degree that they will apply their heart for the world. As normal as you make it is as normal as they will think it is. The process of making World Christianity "normal" goes something like this:

Motivation.

Millions of Christian students pass casually through four of the most important years of their life. Many are involved in college ministries and yet they lack vision for the nations. Everything in our culture says, "Look out for number one!" The only stimulants for the average person are financial gain, success, or fear of failure. Very few students have been introduced to the fact that three billion souls are without Christ. Even fewer students realize that their lives can be used to impact the eternal destiny of these people. Imagine if students did know that! What a major alteration in motivation!

So how does it happen? Motivation is often the student's initial exposure to missions and there are a number of ways that can take place. It can be through a speaker at a campus meeting or conference, through a discipler or friend, a video or book. Whatever it takes, the student needs to be exposed to God's heart for the world because motivation is always the first step of mobilization.

Information.

The second step is information. Without it, motivation becomes just another good talk from another great speaker. If all we give the students is motivation, we run the risk of creating "zeal without knowledge" (Prov. 19:2). In our previous scenario the annual missions conference and the trip to New Mexico were the motivation. But they were not followed up with information. I myself am a product of a good speaker that left me with no tools.

For a short time I was passionate about what I'd learned, but quickly my enthusiasm waned. If only he had given me a small amount of follow up, I would have been saved from years of struggle! This same problem is not exclusive to me; it is widespread. Unless we follow students up with information, they will not be equipped to grow on their own.

Your goal in the information stage is to bring the student to a place where he/she is able to develop and cultivate his own World Christian vision. There is a vast amount of information available, but what students will need to know is how to access resources like mission agencies, prayer resources, Bible studies, magazines and books. They will need to know terms like "welcomer," "goer," or "mobilizer," etc. Teach them about world religions and about historical mission movements. Let the student see you utilizing these tools on a consistent basis. This will provide for them a sturdy foundation on which their motivation can grow and equip them with the confidence to move out on their own.

Attention.

"Even after information is given, we still may see very few World Christians raised up. There are plenty of case studies where students have motivation and information and still do nothing. Why is this? Everything around them is pulling for their passion, time and interest. They desperately need personal attention. Even though I know that Jesus Christ is Lord and have submitted myself to Him; I know how to study the Bible, pray and evangelize, that doesn't negate my need for regular accountability. I have all the tools to grow as a Christian, but my tendency, if left alone, is to become lethargic about my Christian walk.

It is the same for anyone seeking to live a World Christian lifestyle. Your goal in giving attention is to guide and prompt the student into continued growth. This happens through steady contact and consistent challenge. Keep world vision in front of the student using some of the suggestions on the list below. This attention will provide support for their growing motivation."

Motivation, information, and attention are critical for anyone desiring to implement missions into their ministry. If you will be committed to the process of raising up World Christians, then you will see students capable of continuing what you have started.

Here is a list of creative ideas to make world vision an integral part of your large or small group ministry. If you were to do one of the following you would have motivated, if you were to choose several others and do them for a few weeks you would have informed, but when these are consistently put into practice you are giving the needed attention for healthy World Christians to grow."

Large Group Meetings

• Start your weekly meeting with a country update and prayer.

• Read a missions book or biography and do an overview at the large group meeting. You may even have copies for people to buy if interested.

• Show a 3-5 minute missions video in your large group meeting to create excitement.

• Have missionaries that are home on furlough give a testimony to the group.

• Have students who have been on short-term trips

give their testimony of how it changed their lives.

- Bring in missions-focused speakers to challenge the students to get personally involved.

- Have an international night where a student of another religion shares for 5-8 minutes about their beliefs.

- Have a place at the meeting for students to give loose change that can be donated to a designated mission or missionary.

- Give regular updates of what God is doing around the world as you read the news and brainstorm how this will affect the gospel in that region.

- Keep a world map in a very visible spot in the meeting room.

- Devote an entire meeting to prayer for the world. Divide the meeting up into small groups and give each one a different country or people group to pray for.

- Host a weekly prayer time at 10:40 for anyone interested in praying for the world.

- Host an international dinner at someone's house and invite internationals from a specific country to cook their culture's food.

Small Group Bible Studies

- Have a Bible study focused specifically on looking up passages that use the words nation, world, peoples or earth in them.

- Memorize key missions passages as a group.

- Pick a New Testament Epistle and read through it in one sitting and make observations about what it says regarding God's heart for the world.

- Find a short missions article and spend the first 15 minutes of Bible study reading and discussing it.

- Create a monthly prayer calendar that focuses on praying for various countries.

- Have someone in the small group research a country and spend the first 10 minutes of your time praying for it as a group.

- Meet internationals on campus and start a prayer list, praying for them by name.

- Hold one meeting focused solely on how to pray for the world and why it is important.

- Have your Bible study take personal interest in a specific country or people group and give financially to a missionary who is currently there.

- Develop accountability among group members that will keep them consistent in the growth of their world vision.

- Subscribe your entire small group to free missions magazines.

- As a group, skip a meal during the day to pray for the hungry in the world.

- Have your Bible study take an international student out on a Friday night, get to know them and show them around.

The Ten Modules

Module 6

How to Cultivate World Prayer

By David Smithers

The purpose of establishing prayer meetings or prayer societies is to create an opportunity and environment where groups of believers can come together to take full advantage of the access and influence they have with God through the sufficiency of Christ. Through the gift of corporate prayer, believers have the privilege of combining their mutual faith and strength in Christ, for the benefit of achieving and enforcing Christ's Kingdom goals. Our combined corporate prayers of faith supernaturally produce better and quicker results than our individual prayers. A biblical reference for the power and potential of corporate prayer is found in Matthew 18:18-20:

> Again I say to you that if two of you agree on earth concerning anything that they ask, it will be done for them by My Father in heaven. For where two or three are gathered together in My name, I am there in the midst of them.

The greater the number united in true faith and prayer, the easier the victory can potentially be won. Just as a team of horses can move a heavy load faster and easier than one horse, so spiritual obstacles can be more quickly overcome by the prayer efforts of a united group, than by the prayers of an individual. The principle of joining forces to maximize our spiritual strength is again clearly seen in Ecclesiastes 4:12: Though one may be overpowered by another, two can withstand him. And a threefold cord is not easily broken.

Consistency in united prayer is born out of a corporate sense of urgency and spiritual hunger. In times of great need, men naturally seek the surest and quickest path to victory. For the Church that path is Christ-centered and faith-filled corporate prayer! "Let us therefore come boldly to the throne of grace, that we may obtain mercy and find grace to help in time of need" (Heb. 4:16). A humble recognition of great need coupled with great faith in Christ will always produce bold and effective prayer. When Jesus was moved with compassion upon seeing the great need of the multitudes, He urged His disciples, "The harvest truly is plentiful, but the laborers are few. Therefore pray..." (Matt. 9:36-38).

Spirit-led prayer meetings are birthed out of an understanding that there are multiplied millions of souls that need the multiplied strength of our united prayers! The eternal needs of today's sin-sick world demand that we forsake our small ambitions and petty preferences so we might have the opportunity to band together in prayer. In light of our present needs both in the Church and the world, who among us can argue that we don't have time for corporate prayer? Surely five of us will chase a hundred, and a hundred of us will put ten thousand to flight, if only we will unite in fervent, Christ-centered prayer (Lev. 26:8).

The most familiar scriptural passage addressing corporate prayer in a time of great need is found in 2 Chronicles 7:14: "If My people (as a congregated unit) who are called by My name will humble themselves and pray and seek My face and turn from their wicked ways, then I will hear from heaven, and will forgive their sin and heal their land." This passage gives us both the prescription and description for a genuine revival. In times of great

84

need and apostasy God always prescribes a corporate call to humble and repentant prayer. Biblically and historically, prayer has always been the means of grace to bridge the gap between a great need and a great awakening! In a similar way, Christ, after giving His disciples The Great Commission, charged them to first tarry in united prayer (Luke 24:45-49).

The early Church was birthed and empowered while participating in a corporate prayer meeting (Acts 1:14). Can we improve upon the New Testament pattern of the apostles? Do we honestly believe that we can finish what our Church fathers started without employing the same methods of united, fervent prayer? Let's consider now some of the principles and activities that either strengthen or weaken our potential in the place of united and corporate prayer.

Some Helps to Corporate Prayer:

Appoint a Prayer Leader

One of the most important things needed in starting a prayer society is good leadership. A prayer meeting can be successfully lead by one leader or two or three united prayer leaders. An important quality to look for in any potential prayer leader is his or her ability to facilitate and encourage prayer in other people. Good prayer leaders are not content to do all the praying themselves. A good prayer leader is someone who can both inspire and also naturally encourage young Christians to pray out publicly. It has been said that prayer is better caught than taught.

Therefore, don't make the mistake of selecting a prayer leader based strictly upon their ability as a good public speaker or Bible teacher. Remember, not everyone who seems to be gifted in communicating well with other people, necessarily has the skills or faith to communicate well with God. A good prayer leader doesn't just lecture on prayer; he models prayer. Above all, a good prayer leader is someone who is already established and growing in the practice of daily prayer and worship. A wise leader casts vision, brings direction and accountability, and when necessary gently corrects those who would use the prayer meeting for their own agenda.

Establish a Consistent Meeting Place

All of us are creatures of habit: we seem to function better in familiar surroundings. When starting a corporate prayer meeting it is very important to keep this in mind. We all have some kind of regular habits and routines that help us get our daily duties accomplished. We have fixed places and set times and appointments. We have offices, desks, classrooms and personal equipment. All of these physical things and surroundings help us to mentally engage in our everyday jobs. Unconsciously, all of us are being continually prompted to behave in very specific ways by our physical surroundings. Familiar places trigger familiar practices! Understanding this simple fact about ourselves will help us to establish a stronger corporate prayer meeting. You can help make it easier for people to enter into corporate prayer by simply establishing a fixed meeting place.

Familiar surroundings help people to feel more comfortable and less guarded. Constant change can create an atmosphere of stress and uneasiness. Therefore, try not to allow the location and time of your prayer meeting to be moved unnecessarily. Inconsistency and frequent changes, either in your meeting place or meeting time will hinder any group of people from becoming quickly established in the practice of corporate prayer!

Unity and Agreement with Christ

Prayer is not merely a monologue but a divine dialogue between God and His children. Prayer happens when believers humbly bring their needs and faith in direct contact with God's grace and promises of provision. This marriage between human need and sovereign provision naturally demands a strong foundation of unity and agreement. "Now this is the confidence that we have in Him, that if we ask anything according to His will, He hears us" (1 John 5:14). Not only must the words of our request be in line with God's revealed will for our corporate prayers to be effective, but also the course and direction of our lives. John 15:7 says, "If you abide in Me, and My words abide in you, you will ask what you desire, and it shall be done for you."

Effective prayer is dependent upon our submission and unity with Christ's eternal purposes. We cannot expect for our prayer meetings to be blessed if we are not going the same direction as Jesus! We are reminded of this truth again in Psalm 66:18, "If I regard (or harbor) iniquity in my heart, the Lord will not hear." Prayer is not merely saying all the right words so we can get what we want. The practice of prayer is the overflow and expression of true agreement with God's Kingdom purposes and will for our lives. God will not answer our requests if we are willfully hanging on to the very things that are working against His holy kingdom.

Unity and Agreement with the Body of Christ

The members of Christ's Body share a divine connection as they are rightly related to their Head and King, Jesus Christ. Consequently, effective prayer is not only dependent upon our unity with God, but also with each other. Many have wrongly assumed that any group who asks God for the same thing at the same time satisfies the corporate prayer requirements of Matthew 18:18: "Again I say to you that if two of you agree on earth concerning anything that they ask, it will be done for them..." However, what is being urged here is much more than superficial agreement. 1 John 3:22-23 makes this plain: "And whatever we ask we receive from Him, because we keep His commandments and do those things that are pleasing in His sight. And this is His commandment: that we should believe on the name of His Son Jesus Christ and love one another."

If we are to be effective in corporate prayer we cannot allow loveless envy, strife, and division to go unchecked in our midst. Matthew 5:23-24 again underscores the importance of love and forgiveness in prayer: "Therefore if you bring your gift to the altar, and there remember that your brother has something against you, leave your gift there before the altar, and go your way. First be reconciled to your brother, and then come and offer your gift." (Also look at 1 Peter 3:7.) Are we serious about establishing corporate prayer? Then we must learn how to live with the roof off and the walls down, nothing between God and us and nothing between each other!

Praise and Worship

Praise and worship can contribute in many different ways to a corporate prayer meeting. The singing of worship choruses and hymns helps people sharpen their faith and focus on Jesus Christ. The greater our corporate vision of Christ, the less we will struggle with distractions and disunity in prayer.

A. W. Tozer once said, "One hundred pianos all tuned to the same fork are automatically tuned to each other. They are of one accord by being tuned, not to each other, but to another standard to which each one must individually bow. So are one hundred worshippers meeting together, each one looking away to Christ..." Worship brings people into greater agreement with God and as a result, greater agreement with each other. Jesus when teaching on prayer exhorted his disciples to approach the throne of grace with worship (Matt. 6:9). Not only should we start our meetings with worship, but we must recognize worship as an aid in facilitating a greater amount of intensity in intercession throughout our prayer meetings.

Eventually in every prayer meeting there will be a time when everyone has prayed all that they know to pray. Often this is when many prayer meetings are prematurely drawn to a close and dismissed. If a prayer group will learn how to refocus on Christ through brief times of intermittent worship, usually fresh direction and a renewed burden to pray will follow.

When we allow ourselves to become passive spectators, we put an incredible strain on the overall focus of the prayer meeting. Worship gives us a practical way of staying mentally engaged and involved in the prayer meeting. This is especially helpful when attempting to have an all-night prayer meeting. Mixing worship into your times of prayer will help you spend a larger amount of time in the presence of God.

Let me add one caution concerning incorporating worship into your prayer meeting - corporate worship is not a substitute for corporate prayer! Be careful not to allow your times of worship to prevent you from making quality time for prayer. True worship should always facilitate prayer, not replace it.

Persistence in Prayer

A healthy prayer society knows how to pray through and fully release what God puts on their heart. Pushing through in persistent faith and repeated prayer is the key to releasing a God-given burden. Many believers have been wrongly taught that to pray more than once about something is a lack of true faith. However, Jesus Himself persistently prayed three times in the garden of Gethsemane before He found relief for His burdened heart (Matt. 26:44). The apostle Paul also prayed three times about his thorn in the flesh before he found God's comfort –"My grace is sufficient for you" (2 Cor 12:8-9; look also at Luke 18:1-8 and 2 Kings 4:17-37).

91

There seems to be an unspoken rule among some prayer groups that after one prayer, a matter should be closed and set aside for the rest of the meeting. Nevertheless, many times there still remains someone with a nagging urge to pray again for the same need or topic. It is then that the voice of human reasoning often slips in and says, "They have already prayed for that need, and you don't want to push it, so just leave it alone." Some matters only need to be prayed for once and the burden is lifted and done with, while other things need to be prayed for repeatedly before the burden is fully released. Regardless of the amount of times, the prayer burden needs to be discharged before moving on to another topic.

The designated prayer leader or leaders must learn how to be sensitive to the Spirit of prayer and when necessary slow the meeting down so everyone has a chance to thoroughly pray through each topic. This will help the prayer meeting to move in a straight line and come to natural conclusion. Such persistent and careful praying instills within the participants a sense of spiritual progress and accomplishment. When we ignore these promptings to pray, we often miss the best time to lift up a particular petition before the whole prayer group. Then on occasion when someone attempts to recover that missed opportunity the whole group is forced to suddenly move backward. This usually causes the prayer meeting to jump back and forth, losing focus and momentum. A good prayer meeting should build and grow in intensity, moving from one prayer topic to another until it concludes with a sense of victory and accomplishment. God loves to confirm the things that are close to His heart through persistent and repeated prayer.

The Benefit of Vocal Prayer

The benefits of persistent prayer previously mentioned are largely dependent upon our willingness to pray out vocally so that those around us can hear what we are praying. Many sincere Christians however, are greatly intimidated when encouraged to pray out-loud in front of others. They rationalize their fears, assuring themselves that their silent prayers are just as effective as someone's vocal prayers. If everyone only prayed silently, what would our prayer meetings be like? No one is suggesting that silent prayer is not legitimate in its proper place.

A consistent prayer meeting will naturally experience variations in outward expression and levels of intensity. There will be prolonged seasons of waiting in silence and other times when everyone is loudly crying out, all at the same time. Still, the best benefits of a corporate prayer meeting usually come when each individual believer lifts their voice to God in prayer one at a time. The reason for this is that silent prayer is much more subject to distractions. All of us have attempted to pray silently, only to realize later that we had not been praying at all, but merely entertaining random thoughts. Praying out audibly helps to prevent this from happening.

Vocal prayer will help anyone attempting to pray either corporately or privately to direct their thoughts and focus towards God. Expressing ourselves through vocal prayer brings direction and corporate agreement, and encourages unity with all those praying around us. Often times God uses our vocal prayers to confirm within other believers the leadership of the Holy Spirit. How many people are missing out because we choose to choke back the yearnings and utterances of our praying heart!

The Potential of Prayer

God has placed before us an open door of limitless power and potential through the means of intercessory prayer. That is, if we grasp by faith what the Lord has already promised and placed in our hands. Regardless of your age, education, race, or gender, God is eagerly waiting to use your prayer life to change the world! You may not be gifted to preach or teach in the Church, but you can touch multitudes of hungry souls through the power of prayer. You may be bedridden and unable to travel, but through Christ-centered prayer you can reach the darkest corners of an unreached and sin-sick world. You may have never been to Bible college or seminary, but through prayer you have the opportunity to influence thousands of lives for Christ. You may be despised and rejected as a "nobody" in the eyes of the world, but through faith in Christ you have the privilege of accepting the Spirit's invitation to come boldly to the throne of grace.

Isn't this what Jesus is encouraging us do in John 15:5-7? He declares, "I am the vine, you are the branches. He who abides in Me, and I in him, bears much fruit; for without Me you can do nothing...If you abide in Me, and My words abide in you, you will ask what you desire, and it shall be done for you." God Almighty has opened a door to every believer, regardless of class or distinction, which leads to the most potentially fruitful ministry of all ministries—prayer.

Prayer not only levels the spiritual playing field between every class, race, and gender, but it also gives each believer immediate and unlimited access to the sovereign King of Glory. Through prayer all men everywhere can intimately touch the heart of God anytime and anywhere! When someone hears a message about the gospel starved millions, they don't have to wait to do something about it. They can immediately get on their knees and apply the message they have heard. They don't have to wait to get special training or raise financial support before they can do something with what they've heard. They can immediately go to prayer and labor on behalf of those who have never heard the good news of Jesus Christ.

Through prayer we can disarm the power of delayed obedience and spiritual procrastination. Through prayer we can each make a difference. Prayer opens prison doors and preaching doors. Prayer binds the enemy and opens the heavens. Prayer is the plow that breaks up the fallow ground for the Gospel seed. Prayer ushers in the glory of the Kingdom of Jesus Christ. Therefore, is there really any such thing as a Christian who genuinely loves the souls of men who fails to passionately pray?

Let us pray big, fully assured that the God to whom we pray is bigger still. After conquering France, Napoleon declared himself Emperor and set out to overtake the rest of Europe. As his forces moved into the Mediterranean he knew one particular island would be costly to invade. Laying siege to the island Napoleon's army suffered many casualties. In celebration of the victory, Napoleon dined with his generals. During the dinner a young soldier entered the room and approached the Emperor's table. Shocked by the boldness of the soldier to approach his Emperor, the generals stood to remove him. Napoleon looked at the battle-worn soldier and asked his purpose. He turned and faced Napoleon and simply said, "Napoleon, give me this island." The soldier's audacious request shocked the whole room. Without saying a word Napoleon summoned for a piece of paper and something to write with. It took a few seconds for Napoleon to write his response. The soldier read the note, thanked him, and walked out.

The generals waited in anticipation. "I granted his request," Napoleon finally said. Astonished, the other men murmured among themselves as to this young soldier's identity. Napoleon hushed them all, "The reason I gave him the island was that I was honored by the magnitude of the request." As we pray, we should strive to do the same: to honor God by the magnitude of our requests, knowing that His power is limitless.

Module 7

How to Handle Excuses

Have you heard the latest statistics? They are sobering:

- *China has 1 Missionary for every 700,000 people*

- *India: 1 Missionary for every 2 million people*

- *Indonesia: 1 Missionary for every 68,000 people*

- *Pakistan: 1 Missionary for every 213,000 people*

- *Bangladesh: 1 Missionary for every 250,000 people*

- *Japan: 1 Missionary for every 26,000 people*

- *Vietnam: 1 Missionary for every 2 million people*

- *Russia: 1 Missionary for every 140,000 people*

- *Iran: 1 Missionary for every 3 million people*

- *Turkey: 1 Missionary for every 270,000 people*

- *America: 1 missionary for every 2,700 people*

I have asked myself many times why this is. Why does the world still look like this even though we have had 2,000 years since Christ gave His Great Commission? There are as many answers to that question as there are people. But the obvious conclusion must be that it is not God's fault: it is ours. We have allowed God's agenda to take a back seat to ours. As soon as you start challenging students to take seriously the redemption of all nations, you have entered sacred territory. You are threatening the very core of their life purpose, and that kind of thing doesn't give too easily. They have spent much time, money, and energy planning the most efficient fulfillment of their dreams, and you are confronting them with a crossroads. So get ready, here they come...the excuses. They come in all shapes and sizes and most people are committed to them, so if you are going to impart missions vision to people, you must be prepared to combat these excuses. We've collected a list of some of the most popular ones along with some handy tips for countering and disarming them.

"But what about my debt?"

For every $1 an American makes, he spends $1.10. This is not good. With credit card booths in the student center and the price of tuition on the rise, debt is an ever-lurking evil for the average college student. It is a real issue! Many students upon graduation are already starting with $10,000 of debt. Many students wish their debt was as small as $10,000! How Christian college students deal with the subject of missions will be seriously affected by their debt situation. Some will use their debt as an automatic excuse to never go overseas; some will procrastinate their involvement until they get it taken care of. So what do you tell them? Should they expend even more money to go on a short-term mission trip this summer or focus on getting out of debt? The initial reaction to this question is usually an emphatic *no* to going overseas, but there are a few options. First, many students are not motivated to get out of debt and therefore find themselves incurring more. Maybe what would motivate them is to go overseas on a short term trip. Many times a small glimpse of the reality of world poverty will cure any lethargy about getting out of debt and any carelessness about standard of living. Another option is to raise not only the necessary money for the trip, but to also raise an extra sum of money to cover expenses while on the trip. For example, if a trip is $2,500 and lasts a month, why not raise an extra $800-$1,000 to offset the amount you could have earned if you had stayed home and worked? If car or housing payments are the issue, the same would apply. A short-term trip is a great motivator to becoming debt free!

What about longer-term? Is that even an option? Yes. I know of a girl who had a $400-a-month debt payment after graduation but felt strongly that she should go to the Middle East to reach Muslims. Her debt was a roadblock. She asked her mission agency if it would be ok to raise above and beyond the support needed so she could offset the cost of her debt every month. They agreed. She asked two people to give $200 a month specifically toward her debt and found that people were more than happy to do it! To them, this $200 a month was the best investment they could make. This is not a way to shove off the consequences of irresponsible spending and should not be taken advantage of, but it is a viable way for people who sincerely desire to serve overseas to be freed from the bondage of debt. Debt is a real issue, but it is not a valid excuse.

"But I don't have that kind of money."

Not many college students have $3,000 tucked in their savings waiting to be spent at a moment's notice on a mission trip. So what do you do when someone tells you they can't go overseas because they don't have any money? First, help them to understand that their mission trip is totally and completely free. You're probably thinking, "Wait a minute; I thought you just said it was a $3,000 trip!" Well it is, but they need to understand the Biblical concept of raising support. In Matthew 10:9-10 Jesus talks about how the worker is worthy of his wage, and Paul the Apostle echoed this when he talked about the privilege he had to raise support in 1 Corinthians. 9:1-18. So the trip is free for them because God has set up an economy where His Body supports those who go out. It may be an overwhelming concept at first, but it's really quite simple. All they need to do is make a list of people they know, send them a letter of explanation, follow up with a phone call and sometimes schedule a personal appointment to further explain financial needs.

There are only two types of students who refuse to do this: the ignorant and the arrogant. The ignorant are unaware of the fact that the Bible speaks of support raising and that God has placed people in their life who are prepared to give. The arrogant are too prideful to call anyone on the phone and "beg" for money. It is below them to show any sign of need. In fact, it is not begging at all; it is the biblical model set up by God Himself and modeled by Jesus, as we read in Luke 8:3, which lists a support team in early church history: "Joanna the wife of Cuza, the manager of Herod's household; Susanna; and many others. These women were helping to support them out of their own means."

"But I don't feel called."

This is one of the most prevailing excuses around today. The infamous God-hasn't-called-me-overseas line! So how are we to respond to this excuse? First, if you do a word study on the word "called," you will find that the only calling in scripture is the calling to come to Christ for salvation. As a matter of fact, Paul the apostle equated his coming to Christ with his responsibility to reach all nations. Listen to what he says to the Galatians in the first chapter of his letter (vv. 15-16): "But when God, who set me apart from birth and called me by His grace, was pleased to reveal

His Son in me so that I might preach him among the Gentiles (nations)." Paul understood he had a general obligation to take the gospel to all nations simply because God had extended salvation to him. Second, when Paul received a "call" into a specific place for ministry, it was while he was actively ministering and fasting (Acts 13:1-4). Most people, while lamenting, "I am not called," are just using that as an escape and are far from ministering and fasting before God to find direction. Oh, and by the way, the last verse in Acts 12 talks about how Paul had just returned from his first mission trip! Apparently, Paul thought it best to be obedient to the purpose of God in the world instead of being hung up on the specifics. So next time someone says he doesn't feel called, just ask him how many mission trips he has been on, what he is doing for the Lord right now, and how often he is fasting about the decision.

"But my parents would never let me go."

Let's just admit it; historically, we have made some bad decisions. Everyone has! It's a part of growing up! As true as this is, it is also true that parents have seen every single one of our lousy choices... dating and breaking up with all the wrong people, discontentment with cars and jobs, changing majors three times or more, and the list goes on. And now a mission trip for the summer in North Sudan! Sounds like another bad idea to Mom and Dad. Can we blame them?

There are really two types of parents who say no to their child going on a mission trip: those who mean it and those who don't. There are some parents who say, "If you go on this mission trip, don't bother coming home ever again, and plan on paying for your car and college when you get back." In this case I would highly advise waiting until they are a little more softened to the idea. Tell the student to heed the advice of their parents while they are under their authority. In the meantime, they can spend their summer reaching out to internationals in the community.

The other parent says no as more of a smoke screen to see if their child is serious or if it's just a passing phase. The difference with this type of parent is that as they are kept informed about their child's life, and they watch him take responsible steps toward the trip and grow increasingly interested, they grow in confidence of their child's decision and will eventually concede. Most parents fall into the latter category. Be careful that the student using his parents as an excuse is not hiding behind a situation that doesn't really exist.

There is a balance in Scripture that God desires us to have, and we must be careful not to be extreme and one-sided. The balance is between Exodus 20:12, "Honor your father and your mother," and Luke 14:26, "If anyone comes to me and does not hate his father and mother, his wife and children, his brothers and sisters - yes, even his own life - he cannot be my disciple." How do these two passages co-exist? I think what God is saying is that there is a way to honor our parents, heed their advice, and still follow God's will over our parents' will. Generally, the cultural transition point from submission to independence happens at college graduation. Usually at this time a person is viewed as "on his own." It's rare to hear 30-40 year old saying, "I would go overseas, but my parents won't let me." They are making their own decisions.

The key is helping the student genuinely try to understand from their parents' perspective. Explain that it is hard for them to let their child go into a potentially dangerous, seemingly irresponsible, and certainly expensive situation with their full consent! Encourage the student to respectfully discern God's path for them, spending much time before the Lord, and seeking a lot of counsel.

"But I am not ready spiritually to go."

When I was in college, this is the one I fell

106

back on. I was challenged to give my summer to reaching out to the Muslims in North Africa for eight weeks by an individual who was a missions zealot. My response to him was, "But I am not ready to go!" He didn't hesitate with his response, "Ok, I'll give you 20 minutes...get ready." "What, no wait! I don't think you understood what I meant!" I thought. In reality, he understood me perfectly.

So how will you respond? You might begin by asking the student what he is waiting for, what will make him feel ready. If it is truly an issue of spiritual maturity and he is neglecting the spiritual disciplines, then be prepared to walk him through the basics of Bible study, prayer, and evangelism. Often, however, he is waiting to become sinless, to have totally pure motives, or to love the people as Christ does! If that's the case, he will never be "ready." Missionaries are real people that have real problems. No one reaches a certain spiritual state and then becomes qualified. Actually, the process works in the reverse order. Once a person goes and catches a real vision for the nations and realizes the incredible task at hand, he will see an increased intimacy with Christ. If the goal before us is small, our dependence on the Lord will be small. On the other hand, if our aspirations are great, our reliance on the sufficiency of God will be great. One missions leader even says if someone has been a

Christian for longer than 8 weeks, they are qualified.

Encourage the student to not let his feelings of insufficiency keep him from the field; he is just the kind of candidate the Lord is looking for: "But God chose the foolish things of the world to shame the wise; God chose the weak things of the world to shame the strong" (1 Corinthians 1:27).

"But I don't really have a heart to go."

When a person comes at you with this excuse, help him to see what the natural state of man is without Christ. Here are some of the descriptions found in the New Testament: dead in trespasses and sins, lost, blind, selfish, enemy of God, living for the lust of flesh, indulging in the desires of flesh, a child of wrath, walking according to the ways of the devil, unable to understand, useless, deceitful, bitter, destructive, miserable, without fear of God, incurring the wrath of God—and this is just a sampling. The person above is totally unable to have a heart for the world like God does. However, when a person accepts Christ something happens. Ezekiel explains it this way: "I will sprinkle clean water on you, and you will be clean; I will cleanse you from all your impurities and from all your idols. I will give you a new heart and put a new spirit in you; I will remove from you your heart of stone and give you a heart of flesh. And I will put my

108

Spirit in you and move you to follow my decrees and be careful to keep my laws" (Ezek. 36:25-27). The salvation experience involves a change of heart. The heart that formerly could not care for the world and its lost, thrived on selfishness, and craved sin was taken out and in its place the Lord put a heart of flesh. Now it is possible to care, love, give, and go. That heart is already in any Christian; all that needs to be done is cultivation. So when someone says, "But I don't really have a heart to go," our response should be, "Yes, you do if you're a believer...just cultivate it by praying, giving, going short term, and reaching out to internationals on campus."

"But what about the needs here?"

This is another very common excuse that you may run into. I usually answer it with the example of triage. It is a medical term that means that those who have the worst injuries get priority over other injuries. So if someone comes in the emergency room with a leg that has been cut off, he will take priority over the person who is waiting with a sprained ankle. Why is that? Do the doctors love the person with the severed leg more than the sprained ankle? Of course not. His need is more urgent and therefore takes priority. What if we appropriated that to missions, implementing a missionary triage? Its application would be simple:

those with the greatest need, the least reached, and those without a church would get priority over those cultures with established churches. Keith Green, a zealous musician who recruited for missions, said, "Since America has only about 5% of the world's population, then only about 5% of the believers would really be called to stay in this country as a witness (that's only about 1 out of 20) while the rest of us should go into the parts of the world where there are almost 0% believers." Unfortunately, that is not the case. On the contrary, 95% of believers will stay within the United States. Are there needs in the United States? Without a doubt. It is impossible to walk around a college campus in America without seeing the need for more Christian laborers. But there's one thing to remember—there will always be a need in America. Needs are everywhere. Maybe it's time to stop focusing on the needs and instead focus on the greatest need— those with no gospel access.

We need to make sure that our definition of missions aligns correctly with God's. In Revelation 5:9 God gives us His definition of missions: "And they sang a new song: 'You are worthy to take the scroll and to open its seals, because you were slain, and with your blood you purchased men for God from every tribe and language and people and nation.'" His goal is to have a representative from every tribe, tongue, and nation and therefore, missions is our participation in the completion of this goal. All of our efforts, energy, money, and time need to be poured into seeing this become a reality. John Piper in his book *Let the Nations Be Glad* gives a wonderful illustration of this very point:

Suppose there were two ocean liners on the sea, and both began to sink at the same time with large numbers of people on board who did not know how to swim. There are some lifeboats, but not enough. And suppose you were in charge of a team of ten rescuers in two large boats.

You arrive on the scene of the first sinking ship and find yourself surrounded by hundreds of screaming people, some going down before your eyes, some fighting over scraps of debris, others ready to jump into the water from the sinking ship. Several hundred yards farther away the very same thing is happening to the people on the other ship.

Your heart breaks for the dying people. You long to save as many as you can. So you cry out to your two crews to give every ounce of energy they have. There are five rescuers in each boat and they are working with all their might. They are saving many. There is lots of room in the rescue boats. Then someone cries out from the other ship, 'Come over and help us!' What would love do? Would love go or stay? I cannot think of any reason that love would leave its life-saving labor and go to the other ship. Love puts no higher value on distant souls than on nearer souls. In fact, love might well reason that in the time it would take to row across the several hundred yards to the other ship, an overall loss of total lives would result... Love may not see the missionary task the way God does. God may have in mind that the aim of the rescue operation should be to gather saved sinners from every people in the world (from both ocean liners), even if some of the successful rescuers must leave a fruitful reached people (the first ocean liner), in order to labor in a (possibly less fruitful) unreached people (the second ocean liner). In other words, the task of missions may not be merely to win as many individuals as possible from the most responsive people groups of the world, but rather to win individuals from all the people groups of the world.

It is imperative that our definition of and participation in missions are not dictated by culture or by human reason. God has a plan and it includes every nation! Help the student to see the difference between God's ultimate desire and man's logic. The reason for his struggle with the needs in America may be rooted in a lack of knowledge of the world's needs. The point is not that staying in America and ministering here is second-class. That is a perfectly legitimate need. But in all we do, the underlying purpose ought to be the total fulfillment of God's mission.

"But isn't it better to send my money?"

In today's world economy and the increasing value of the American dollar, sending money instead of people has become a very alluring option. I was at an appointment with an affluent pastor. We were on the subject of missions, and I was challenging him to consider giving to our ministry. His response took me off guard. He said that neither he nor his church were supporting Americans because their dollar goes a lot further when given to a native worker. It makes sense, and I'm sure this pastor's intention was to make a wise economic decision, but is it a healthy perspective? For some, it may serve as an attempt to justify a lack of involvement. Here are some of the experts' tips on the issue: Robertson McQuilkin, former President of Columbia Bible College and Seminary, in his article "Should We Stop Sending Missionaries?" says:

In most cases, sending just a portion of our surplus $50-$100 each month will provide support for one full-time national worker. The typical cost to send an American missionary family overseas is over $50,000 a year: the same cost as supporting 50 or more national workers. Think of what that money *could do for the Kingdom of God! Admittedly, this rationale is appealing. Nationals have the language and the culture and they cost so much less. More than 140 organizations are now built on the premise of gathering and sending money, not people. But what about the dark half of the world where there are no 'nationals,' no witnessing church? At least a billion of the lost live among a people where there is no evangelizing church movement, often no witness at all. For these, by definition, someone must leave home to reach them. If a foreigner doesn't go in from the outside they'll never hear the Gospel. The fundamental premise of the 'send money, not people' movement is misguided because there are no nationals to reach these billion people even if money were sent.*

Jerry Rankin, former president of the International Mission Board, Southern Baptist Convention, puts it this way:

It is a mistake to try to accelerate growth by an infusion of financial aid to build churches and support pastors. One thing inevitably occurs when North Americans subsidize the work of churches and pastors on the mission field: potential growth is stalled because of a mind-set that it can't be done unless an overseas benefactor provides the funds. Jealousy often develops among the pastors and churches that don't receive assistance toward those who develop a pipeline of support from the United States. In the long-term, support breeds resentment, especially if the support is not sustained indefinitely, because it creates a patronizing dependency. People are deprived of growing in faith, learning to depend on God and discovering that He is sufficient for all their needs.

Robertson McQuilkin has lists six warning signs in supporting nationals:

- Believers learn to depend neither on God nor on themselves because they have no need to give sacrificially of their own resource.

- Leaders become preoccupied with raising North American funds. On a trip I took to India I was overwhelmed by the many who "worked" me for a dollar connection.

- They come to believe that the work can't be done without outside assistance, so why try?

- Believers sue believers. In India, I was astounded to find few churches or ministries that weren't in the courts at war over property purchased using American dollars.

- An independent and unaccountable higher class of Christian workers arises whose stylish life-styles are envied by "unconnected believers."

- Recipients become ungrateful. The ingratitude can take a number of forms: "Sure, you gave us something, but look how much you still have;" or, "It's not yours anyway; you owe it to us."

Rick Wood, former editor of Mission Frontiers Magazine says:

Many churches in the U.S. have bought into this scheme as a way of getting more 'bang for their missions buck.' But what they don't realize is that this 'bargain basement' approach to missions is going to blow up in their faces creating a dependency on the mission field to foreign funds that is deadly to the vibrant, reproducing church planting movements that we want to see within every people. Every church and every people has the God-given privilege and responsibility of supporting its own ministry and cross-cultural outreach. Foreign money robs these peoples of the incentive to give of their lives and resources to support the ministries of their own churches.

So isn't it better to send money? Obviously, not always. The Great Commission still stands today as it did 2,000 years ago: Matthew 28:19 says, "Therefore, go and make disciples of all nations, baptizing them in the name of the Father and of the Son and of the Holy Spirit." Jesus did not give a qualification that says "unless you feel sending a check is better!"

"But isn't the mission field dangerous?"

The Israelites were faced with an interesting choice after leaving their slavery in Egypt. As they got to the edge of the land that God had told them to possess, they began to count the cost of obedience. The land was inhabited by fierce, giant-size men! They found themselves questioning God's command, His promise, and His deliverance from Egypt. All of a sudden disobeying God and returning to slavery seemed more appealing in light of the danger and certain death that awaited them. Here is their response: "Why is the Lord bringing us into this land, to fall by the sword? Our wives and our little ones will become plunder; would it not be better for us to return to Egypt?" (Numbers 14:3). Keith Green explains:

It is all a matter of our priorities - do we look at the temporary or the eternal in making our choices? It's true that you will probably be in more physical danger on the mission field than you would be in the suburbs of America, but that is part of the cost that

117

we need to count when it comes to serving God. The question should not be, 'Will I be kept safe wherever I go?' but rather, 'What is on the Lord's heart for me to do?' If Jesus decided to go the way of least pain, He would have never gone to the cross. There is no place of greater blessing for you than in the center of God's will. You must stop to count the cost, but remember one thing—the privilege of serving God always outweighs the price."

This is only going to grow as an issue because of the increase in wars, threats of wars, kidnappings, and terrorism. You must be mobilizing students to not turn back. The measure of a man is what it takes to stop him. What will it take to stop you? Are you setting the example? Take the students back to the Word, and look toward those who have gone before and made their life a living sacrifice. There is no promise of safety and the dangers are real, but His grace is sufficient for us.

"I am not ready for that kind of sacrifice."

This is the root of all excuses: abstaining from sacrificial living. For some people, when they come to Christ they just Christianize the things they did before. Their logic goes something like this: "I was going to be a teacher, so now I guess I am a Christian teacher. I was going to be a engineer, so now I guess I am a

Christian engineer." It is easy to just add Christ to our pre-existing plans. Those who come with this excuse have most likely fallen into this trap. Therefore, the mindset becomes, "Why would I want to go to the mission field? That is serious sacrifice!" In 2 Corinthians 5:17 we read, "Therefore, if anyone is in Christ, he is a new creation; the old has gone, the new has come!" Notice the key phrase, "the old has gone." This means that all we desired and lived for under our own lordship is done away with. Jesus becomes Lord to guide us in His agenda, not just offer us council about our agenda. This is the minimum, the entry level of commitment, not an elite, super-spiritual commitment that few attain to. Jesus challenges us to consider the cost of following Him before salvation not after.

Suppose one of you wants to build a tower. Will he not first sit down and estimate the cost to see if he has enough money to complete it? For if he lays the foundation and is not able to finish it, everyone who sees it will ridicule him, saying, 'This fellow began to build and was not able to finish.' Or suppose a king is about to go to war against another king. Will he not first sit down and consider whether he is able with ten thousand men to oppose the one coming against him with twenty thousand? If he is not able, he will send a delegation while the other is still a long way off and will ask for terms of peace. In the same way, any of you who does not give up everything he has cannot be my disciple. (Luke 14:28-33)

Erwin McManus, in his book *An Unstoppable Force* discusses his experience in growing as a new Christian and a confusing amount of "other calls."

Soon I had discovered five levels of callings from God: a calling to be saved, a calling for Jesus to be Lord, a calling to ministry, a calling to home missions, and a calling to foreign missions.... Why are there so many levels of Christian calling in our contemporary Christian community? Where are they found in the biblical text? I have a strange suspicion that the nuances of these "callings" have less to do with theology and more to do with the condition of the church. Paul seemed to think there was only one calling. He writes to Timothy, "So do not be ashamed to testify about our Lord, or ashamed of me his prisoner. But join with me in suffering for the gospel, by the power of God, who has saved us and called us to a holy life – not because of anything we have done but because of his own purpose and grace" (2 Timothy 1:8-9). The Scriptures seem to simplify the process of calling. The one call is to lay your life at the feet of Jesus and to do whatever He asks.

The student who approaches you with this issue is struggling with Christ's Lordship. Challenge him to consider what happened at salvation and to Whom he belongs. Ask him if Christ would be pleased with a lesser sacrifice than what He is calling for.

Final Thoughts:

William Carey, Hudson Taylor, Cameron Townsend, C.T. Studd, Gladys Aylward and Amy Carmichael all had one thing in common – they had reasons not to go. Good reasons. But they all had another thing in common – they thought it a worthwhile cost to pay. They considered everything a loss compared to the surpassing greatness of knowing Christ Jesus their Lord, for whose sake they lost all things. Behind the student's excuse sits the same potential of the greats who have gone before. Be a living example of the supreme worth of Christ and be prepared to disarm any excuse that threatens it.

Module 8

How to Mobilize Your Church

By Todd Ahrend

The Church is very close to the heart of God. It was bought by the blood of Christ (Acts 20:28) and is His instrument for redeeming all nations. It is so critical for any missions mobilizer to be committed to the Church and to hold it in high esteem. Part of being committed to the Church means that you do not allow your heart for the nations to come before it. If your church does not share the same convictions about the nations that you hold, don't separate from it: mobilize it.

Paul Borthwick, author and speaker, explains a few reasons why the local church is primary in the Great Commission.

The local church is primary in world missions because Jesus said it is. The promise of Jesus to Peter (Matthew 16:18) states that He will build His church and the gates of hell will not prevail against it. The image is one of a forceful organization of believers representing one Kingdom on the march against another. When the gates of that second kingdom—hell—are attacked, they will fall. Who is supposed to be on this attack? Jesus says it's His Church. For each of us, this manifests itself in the local assembly of believers. The church fails in its task when it loses the mentality of advancement. The missions-minded person who sees this happening in his or her local church should get involved and try to influence church thinking. Without our involvement, the local church will plunge deeper into a fortress-mentality, the missions-minded will become more cynical about the local church, and we all will move further from Jesus' promise that His Church will defeat the gates of hell.

"[Secondly] The local church is primary because the Body of Christ is there. Peer groups and campus fellowships can be wonderful stimuli towards discipleship, and missions but they do not present the

whole cross-section of the body of Christ. The fuller representation of the body of Christ we call the local church also puts us in the presence of older believers whose accumulated wisdom will be our training ground for realistic ministry—in this culture or another."

"[Third] The local church is primary because it affords us training and care. Do you have the patience needed to persevere for years in a Muslim culture without seeing anyone become a Christian? No one really knows, but ministry to the junior high students at the local church can certainly help develop patience. Will you desire to lead people in another culture to Christ, disciple them, and encourage them to be "World Christians"? If you plan to do this, you should take every opportunity to test your skills, methods, and relational abilities right in your own church."

When the groundwork has been laid and the importance of the church is seen with the right perspective, the misconceptions about the church and missions are also laid bare. Bill Stearns in his workbook *A Sunday for the World* explains that most churches have a perspective that Jesus, in Acts 1:8, told His disciples that they would be His witnesses first in Jerusalem, then Judea, then Samaria, then the uttermost parts of the earth. People tend to interpret this as the stages of missions involvement. This is a common error and can be detrimental to the growth of one's missions vision. Stearns says, "Sometimes we think that any attention paid to the uttermost parts of the earth has to wait until we've first perfected our Jerusalem, Judea and Samaria. Although it's true that the strengthening of the local church is foundational to ministry, its not true that we can't concern ourselves with other cultures until our own is fully redeemed."

Jesus told us to be witnesses simultaneously in Jerusalem, Judea, Samaria, and the uttermost parts of the earth. Another malfunction of our single-vision mission is neglect of the local church. A fellowship might concentrate on blessing an unreached people but neglect strengthening its base.

As a mission mobilizer, you must be aware that though it is true that you may have more zeal than others in your church, this does not give you the right to be arrogant and prideful. Your attitude needs to be one of willingness to serve the Body. Be teachable and make sure you get an adequate amount of information so that you do not appear to make blind accusations of your church. Stearns explains the potential ramifications of a wrong attitude or approach to church mobilization: "Often missions activist groups feel a clear sense of purpose and direction, but they are frustrated by lack of prayer power, financial power, and manpower. In frustration, these folds begin to point fingers at the lack of vision of the pastor, the elders, or the rest of the congregation for their obvious selfishness."

Once you feel like your heart is in the right place on the issue, you are ready to get started. First, find one or two people in your church that share your vision for missions. It will be helpful (but not necessary) to have their support as you attempt to mobilize the church.

Most churches have somewhere in their overall purpose statement something about their vision for outreach. Do a little research and find out what that vision is and how it is actively being carried out.

Other things to find out:

- What percentage of funds is given to missions?

- How many missionaries are supported?

- How often is contact made with these missionaries?

- How often is the congregation presented with facts about their own missionaries?

- Is there any emphasis on praying for the world?

- What sources are used for information about the world?

If there is no missions committee in place, your elder board or pastor will be an asset in your researching. As you learn, be thinking of some creative ways to implement missions. Also, pray through the various existing ministries and ask God to show you how they can be used to fuel His global purpose.

Here are a few ideas:

- Put up a bulletin board in a high-traffic area of the church and update it weekly or monthly with a new unreached people group and its specific prayer requests.

- Begin a prayer meeting that meets regularly and is dedicated solely to praying for the nations.

- If there already is a prayer meeting, supply the leaders with information on the unreached and ask them to give time each week to those prayer needs.

- Ask the pastor if once every six months there could be a concert of prayer for the nations.

- Invite individuals in the congregation to "adopt" one of their own missionaries, write them regularly and report to the rest of the church on their needs and prayer requests.

- If your church does not support missionaries, find a mission agency and ask if you can adopt some of their missionaries. (Some mission agencies are geared around linking churches with unreached people groups in such an "adoption" relationship.)

- Get the children's ministries involved by having them make cards to send to missionaries or by taking a coin collection to send to foreign missions.

- Show a missions video in the youth group and spend time praying for missionaries to be sent.

- Take a Saturday and have the congregation go on a vision trip to a part of the community that is predominantly international and host a get-to-know-you picnic or service outreach.

- Invite an international to come and give a testimony in Sunday school about his/her culture and beliefs.

- Organize a summer mission trip for the adults and for the youth using a mission agency.

- Host a fundraiser where everyone can be involved and give the proceeds to overseas missions.

- Host a "Perspectives on the World Christian Movement Course" (www.perspectives.org) and be sure to encourage the pastor and other key leadership to participate.

- Start a Bible study and go through a book of the Bible highlighting God's heart for the nations.

- Have time in the Sunday service to highlight current world news and how that relates to God's heart for the world. Spend time in prayer for those issues.

- Put up a table where free missions resources can always be displayed and available for the congregation (videos, books, magazines, articles, agency brochures, prayer profiles).

- Subscribe your church to several missions' magazines and place them on the resource table.

- Invite members to volunteer in the international department of a nearby college helping students learn English.

- Develop a mission curriculum that people interested in going overseas can go through to become more equipped and prepared.

Once you feel comfortable in your education about the church's policies and well equipped with ideas, it is time to make an appointment to speak with the church leadership. If there is a missions committee, they would be your first preference, followed by the elder board. During this time, share your vision for the nations as well as your vision and specific ideas for the church. Ask for their prayerful advice about where to start and then be prepared to be appointed to the assignment. This will hopefully be the first of many meetings with them. Stay close to your leadership and build a good relationship with them.

Final Thoughts:

Mobilizing your church will be a process, but since it is God's agent to reach the world, it is well worth the effort. As you persevere in being faithful and prayerful, individuals may be raised up to the same vision. If your church is slow to implement new ideas or is unwilling to allow you to participate in their missions development, be ready to offer yourself in another area. The last thing your church needs is someone who is willing only to build a certain agenda and not the whole body. You will validate your message and earn your right to be heard through humility and servanthood.

The Ten Modules

How to Choose the Right Mission Agency

By Todd Ahrend

I was recently at a missions conference where hundreds of agencies were represented. Each displayed their colorful, inviting booths and handed out Snickers bars and the newest attention grabbers—a compass, globe ball, key chain, all kinds of things! I'm sure that those who came to the conference shopping for a mission agency were completely overwhelmed. Worse than that, if they didn't know what they were looking for, they ran the risk of committing to the agency with the most exciting booth or the brochure with the best graphics! There are thousands of mission agencies in existence today. It is so important that the person looking to go on a short or long-term trip knows what to look for when choosing an agency. Think about it – you are going to spend at least two months in a foreign country where you know nothing and no one. On the one hand, people take their vacations very seriously. They want to know where they will be, what the accommodations will be like, what kind of crowd it draws, how much money it will be, how they will get around, if it is in a safe neighborhood, etc. How much more care should be taken in choosing a mission agency or trip?

Many times, students are sidelined from getting involved in missions for one of three reasons: 1) they feel paralyzed by a lack of knowledge about how to move forward, 2) they know one or two options but aren't satisfied with what they offer or 3) they are so overwhelmed with possibilities that they never decide.

When a student approaches you in need of counsel on choosing a mission agency, be prepared with resources. Below is an outline of the process you can walk the student through. It would be helpful for you to do some research in advance and to have in mind agencies you would recommend before you sit down with a student. Help the student to think through places they would like to go or certain experiences they would like to have. For example, if the student is a pre-med major and has a particular interest in Hindus, these two details will narrow down your list of options. If they have no prior interests, that's fine too.

Ultimately, choosing the right agency comes down to research, prayer, and asking the right questions. Be diligent to talk to your church and others who are more experienced. Read magazine articles and even search some good websites before you decide. Give yourself plenty of time to gather research. As you are doing this, the Holy Spirit will guide you as you meet the right people and narrow the choices.

The goal is to collect a wide-range list of mission agencies and their contact information. The first place to begin is talking to your church's missions committee or elder board. Find out if they recommend any particular mission agencies, or if they can help you contact the missionaries that the church supports. If this is a dead end, talk to people who you know have gone and get their input. If you have a campus minister, he or she would likely be an incredible resource in your search. If by now you do not have a healthy list of choices, go to the Internet. You can start at The Traveling Team's website (www.thetravelingteam.org) and go to the Resources page. There you will have the option to click on "mission agencies." The list you will find is made up of agencies that we have thoroughly researched and feel absolutely comfortable endorsing. It is not exhaustive by any means, but it is a good starting point. Now you should have several agencies and a way to contact each of them.

Your next step is to gather the right information from each agency from which you will make your decision. Being a good question asker is an important part of the process.

Here are a few to start with:

- How do they define short term? Long term?

- How will you be funded? Do they have a faith-based policy?

- Will they train you in raising support?

- Do they give an orientation and a debriefing?

- How long have they been a mission agency?

- Do they focus on one specific group, region, or religion?

- What is the deadline for the application to be in?

- Will you be on a team or will they send you by yourself?

- Do you need to be debt free in order to go or do they allow debt?

- Does their doctrine line up with yours? (i.e. Their

stance on spiritual gifts.)

• Can they send some print materials on their agency and on their trip opportunities?

There are many other questions that will come up along the way. Rob Antonucci, former missionary to the Muslim world, has thought through some important things to check into when trying to find the right mission agency:

1. Check out their promotional literature and brochures. Remember this type of literature is only introductory; you still need to ask further questions. Listen to their catch phrases and how they define frequently used terms, such as church-planting, unreached, strategic, teams.

2. Are they working among the Unreached? What does this particular agency mean when they used the word "unreached"? When they say there are no churches in this area, do they mean of their denomination? Does unreached mean they work among those who are non-believers or that they work among those who don't go to the local church? Many are surprised when they get to their "unreached" area and find many workers doing ministry among a host of churches.

3. Are they truly an "international" mission agency? Do they welcome people who are non-North Americans to join? Are nationals or natives equal partners in leadership, planning, and ministry? How does the

agency involve local leadership in the church? Does the mission agency believe in closure, that is, finishing their work and moving to new areas?

4. How does the mission agency work with the local churches and the other mission agencies? How much are they involved in building the kingdom of God versus their own denominational or mission agency churches?

5. What are some of their statistics? What is the source of their data? Is it verifiable? After a mistruth is repeated so many times, it tends to become accepted as fact. Use caution: some statistics are hypothetical, designed for high impact only.

6. Do they use glory stories? All mission agencies are guilty of some misuse of stories of incredible workings of God in a place. For example: "1,000 people converted in one day in country X." Look beneath the surface, get past the headlines, and look for details. Remember, glory stories alone don't necessarily give an accurate picture of what life is like in a particular ministry.

7. How much of an administration fee does a mission take out of the donations for a missionary? Some agencies take less, but offer fewer services. Some take a lot and offer lots of good services for their portion of the donation. Be aware that, if you go with the cheapest mission agency, you might not get some

valuable services that you would with another agency that requires you raise more support.

8. How much of an average missionary's time is spent in ministry versus mission bureaucracy and paperwork? Look closely at the accountability structures. Are missionaries allowed to be completely independent? Are they kept accountable to goals or at least a plan?

9. How willing is an agency to work with your local church? Is your church going to take an active part in the ministry?

Questions 3 and 5-8 may be more appropriate for someone looking to go long-term and are not necessarily of interest to the short-term missionary.

Final Thoughts:

      Consider this story: I once knew a student who had planned a two-week trip to Africa. He was pretty excited about it until I told him about an opportunity to work on the coast of North Africa, reaching the youth who travel there to surf. Come to find out, this student was a pro-surfer! He lit up at the idea of using his love for surfing to reach the lost, but he had already committed himself to Africa. I have no doubt that his time in Africa was invaluable and life-changing, but how much more might he have enjoyed serving the Lord through his love for surfing?

Finding the right agency will play a significant role in the overall mission trip experience. Not only that, but long-term missionaries are born out of short-term missionaries and, many times, the agency used for the short-term is the agency used to go long-term. There are plenty of agencies to choose from; know them and mobilize strategically to them.

Module 10
How to Raise Support
By Steve Shadrach

I want to serve God and be obedient to His leading in my life, but I don't want to....*raise support*! If you have said or thought these words, you are not alone. In fact, most people living a donor-supported lifestyle will admit that at one time they probably had feelings much like this. Although this lifestyle is not a popular one in North America where independence is a high value, it is an essential part of working for many Christian ministries and mission agencies. If God is leading you to a place where support is necessary, it becomes a question of obedience and lordship, not just

140

preference. When that question is answered, support raising just becomes one aspect of the job that God is asking you to do.

Although it can be a difficult obstacle to overcome, many people have come to see it as a blessing. Even though there are stresses and pressures involved in raising and maintaining a personal support team, I would not want to live any other way. The bonds that I have formed over the years with supporters are priceless. I have also had unique opportunities to let God build my faith that I might not have had if I did not raise support. Most of all, when I report to a ministry assignment, there is an added sense of seriousness and professionalism. There are 50+ others that are paying a price to have me ministering there. I had better take it seriously and give it my all. That kind of accountability is invaluable in ministry.

If you are facing an opportunity to raise support, you will probably have some doubts, fears, and questions. You are normal! I still get butterflies each time I pick up the phone to make a support appointment. If you want to be successful you are going to need some guidance. I have listed here five keys to raising your personal support team. This is one of the most exciting adventures that I have ever experienced! So hold on tight and here we go:

The Five Keys to Raising Your Personal Support

1. Understand the Biblical Basis

Take some time to study the Scriptures for yourself so you will know exactly what God thinks about asking others to give to you and to your ministry. A common misconception about support raising is that it is more spiritual to just pray and trust God to bring the funds in. The great George Mueller was led to do this to support his orphanages in 19th century London. But it is just as Biblical and requires as much or more faith to personally invite others to invest. Either way, we have to understand that God is the source of our funds, not the donors, our plans, or our hard work. Scott Morton of The Navigators, in his book, *Funding Your Ministry Whether You're Gifted or Not*, highlights five examples and teachings from the Old and New Testament about the validity of God's ministers being supported by others:

1. The example of the Levites (Numbers 18:24) – The Jews gave their tithe to the priests for support.

2. The example of Jesus (Luke 8:2,3) – Many people supported Jesus and the disciples.

3. The teaching of Jesus (Matthew 10:9,10) – A Kingdom worker is worthy of his support.

142

4. The example of Paul (Acts 18:4,5) – He stopped tent-making to preach full time on support.

5. The teaching of Paul (1 Corinthians 9:1-18) – He had the right to be supported by the churches.

Once you have a biblical perspective on this topic of asking for and living on the support of others, evaluate one more thing: Evaluate your own giving! Before you can ask anyone else to give, you have to be committed to sacrificially investing in Kingdom work on a regular basis. Let's practice what we preach!

2. Kill the Giants in Your Own Mind

The Bible illustrates this interesting principle with the story of the Promised Land. God had already promised that the Israelites would be able to conquer this beautiful land and that He would give them victory over its mighty inhabitants. The Israelites sent twelve Hebrew spies into the Promised Land to take a look before the whole nation was to enter and claim what God had given them. Only two, Joshua and Caleb, came back with a positive report. The other ten spies were so terrified of the giant-sized men they saw in the land that they confessed, "we became like grasshoppers in our own sight, and so we were in their sight." (Exodus 13:33). Instead of trusting God and moving out with courage, they let fear paralyze them.

How they viewed themselves, affected how the giants viewed them. It is the same way in support raising. The confidence level that we have in our God, our vision and ourselves can make us... or break us! All of us have different "giants" in our own minds that will keep us from beginning and persevering in the process of assembling a full support team. These are some common "giants" we must conquer.

- You or your parents might think support raising is really just begging.

- You might think you are not a worthy investment.

- You might think that support raising is just a "necessary evil" that must be endured.

- You might think that people are rejecting you or your ministry if they say no.

You must kill these giants one at a time as you fill your mind with the Scriptures and believe what God has said about you and your calling. Then you can courageously march in and take the land! Just as God had prepared the land for the people to simply go in and take it, we need to believe that God has prepared the hearts of the donors, and we need to walk boldly in faith to find those givers and ask them to join us in our vision.

3. Pray and Plan

Pray! Author S.D. Gordon said it well, "Prayer is the real work of the ministry. Service is just gathering in the results of prayer." We need to bathe our donors and ourselves in prayer before, during, and after this process. God will go before you. He will also give you a love for your donors as you pray for them individually.

Create Your Budget! Include everything you need for your personal needs, giving, saving and ministry expenses. Seek to balance a lifestyle that will allow you to maximize your effectiveness with the group you're reaching, but also be above reproach before your donors in the stewardship of your finances. If you happen to have school debt, simply include the required monthly amount and keep going. Your donors will admire you for keeping your promise to pay it back. Plan on and commit to raising 100% before you report to your assignment. Have a "when I raise my support attitude," not an "if I raise my support."

Namestorm! Write down every person that you have ever known during your lifetime. Don't play Holy Spirit by saying, "Oh, that person would never give." You will be surprised by who gives and who doesn't give! Also, include people that share a heart for the particular area of ministry you are entering. List churches, Sunday School classes, foundations and corporations. The bulk of your support, though, will come from the individuals with whom you meet.

Map Out a Plan! Divide up all the names according to the cities they live in. Then label each name "hot," "cold," or "medium" depending upon whether they probably will give, probably won't give, or they might give. Next, pray and seek to attach an amount that you would like to ask them to give. Don't use a one-size-fits-all plan; instead, base the amount on what you perceive they are able and willing to give along with the kind of relationship you have with them. You might feel more comfortable suggesting a range rather than a specific amount (i.e. from $150-$300). Either way, know that the tendency for most people is to ask for too little, not too much! Remember, there is no cash flow problem in heaven. Americans alone give over 100 billion dollars to charity each year. God has instilled in people a desire to give, and you are helping them to invest in eternal things, building up their treasure in heaven. Go for it!

Plan Out a Map! Figure out what city you will go to first, second, etc. Schedule it out on your calendar. I would suggest sending a letter in advance telling him or her what you are doing and that you will be calling, but the key is to call each person in advance of the trip in order to get the appointment. Don't let them say yes or no to the giving; your only objective is to get an appointment with them. Seek to line up all of your "hot" prospects first, then your "medium" prospects next and finally, your "cold" prospects.

4. Ask them face to face

This is crucial. Jesus said, "we have not because we ask not." The word "ask" is used in the gospels 113 times. God wants to teach us about asking: Him and others. I have looked at surveys as to why people give and the number one reason is always because someone asked them! It is not unspiritual or fleshly to ask. It is biblical, spiritual, and faith-building to ask. Let's not hide behind our fears. Let's walk toward them and render them powerless! The worst thing that they could say is, "No." If you just send a letter out or make a group presentation you might have a 10% response rate. If you send a letter and then call to ask you might get 25% of people to say yes. But, if you are willing to sit down eyeball to eyeball with others and lay out the incredible ministry vision God has called you to, usually well over half of the folks are pulling their checkbooks out! I've had some tell me they have never been turned down in an individual support raising appointment! My research shows that ministries that train their staff to personally ask for the gift raise their full budget in less than half the time of groups that simply share the need, but don't ask. We have not because we ask not.

5. Cultivate the Relationship

Here are the basics for having a long and fruitful relationship with your supporters:

A. Remember it's not fundraising, but "friend raising." You can have an incredible ministry in their lives and you might be their only connection to Jesus Christ or the Great Commission.

B. Consider giving some ministry time to your support team: praying, writing, calling and ministering.

C. Thank before you bank. When a new person joins your team or a new gift comes in, be quick to respond with a thank you card or call. Be prompt and professional in all of your correspondence and record keeping.

D. Regularly send them well-written newsletters. Share how their investments are paying off along with some specific prayer requests. Occasional postcards, phone calls, and visits are great too. Beware: the main reason people drop off of support teams is that they do not hear from their missionary.

E. Win, Keep, Lift. When you win a donor they are now on your team. Keep them on the team by caring for and cultivating them. Periodically, ask them to consider lifting (increasing) their monthly or annual gift to you. Campus Crusade had a campaign where they were asking people to give 1 million dollars to their ministry. Almost 250 people said "yes"! Research showed, though, that the very first gift that each had made to this ministry years earlier had been, on average, a mere $10! Someone had taken the time to win, keep, and (over the years) to lift!

People will stick with you for life if you will appreciate them and keep them informed. View them as vital partners in your ministry and you will gain not only life long supporters, but friends too! One day you will turn around and realize how blessed you have been and that you would not want to live any other way! Trust God and begin this exciting adventure today. You will never regret it!

Getting Practical

Biblical Basis

Is support raising biblical? Look up these verses to gain a proper perspective:

Numbers 18:24, Deuteronomy 12:19, Nehemiah

149

13:10-12, Matthew 10:10, Luke 8:3, Acts 20:33-35, Romans 15:24, Romans 16:1-2, 1 Corinthians 9:3-15, 2 Corinthians 11:8-9, 1 Timothy 5:18, 3 John 5-8

Philosophy

There may still be some doubt in your mind about raising support. Think through how you would answer these questions.

View of GOD: How big is your God? Is He able to provide for all your needs? Is He able to raise up people to join your support team? Can God fail you?

View of SELF: How capable are you? Can God use you? Why would God want to use you? Are you a worthy investment for your supporters?

Why does support raising seem so awkward? Is support raising unbiblical or is it just un-American? Jay Gary says, in his article "Support Raising," that as Americans, "we are supposed to be 'rugged individualists' who refuse handouts and stand on our own two feet. Financial independence is the goal. Some people's problem with raising support, then, is not that it's at odds with any practice in the Bible. Maybe their problem with raising support has more to do with it being counter to the American way of life."

150

Tools

1. Record progress: Use a spreadsheet to keep track of your progress. Record who has been sent a letter, who you have called, who has given you an appointment, and who has received a thank you note. Use this to stay organized. Be accountable to someone.

2. Portfolio: Create a thin folder that visually explains your ministry and needs. Take it on your appointments to help explain your ministry to potential supporters.

3. Prayer: Pray before every support call and appointment. Pray for God's help and provision. He is faithful to those who humble themselves and depend on him.

4. Newsletters: Write a two-page newsletter about yourself to keep people informed in a casual way about your ministry and life, and send it to everyone on your list of current and possible supporters. Be sure to send another one during and/or after your ministry trip.

5. Books: Books that can help you with the concept of support raising are *Friend Raising* by Betty Barnett, *The Support-Raising Handbook: a Guide for Christian Workers* by Brian Rust and Barry McLeish, and *People Raising* by William P. Dillon.

Getting Started

Brainstorm list of names: Think of 50-100 people you can ask for support. This includes family, friends, church members, and anyone else you know. Write a detailed list that includes phone numbers and addresses.

Make practice phone calls: Tell a friend to let you practice on them and pretend it is a support call. Act like you are trying to schedule an appointment.

Plan first few waves of people: Think through the next few weeks and plan which people to ask first. Have about 7-10 people per wave so you don't get too overwhelmed.

Make a newsletter: Write out some stories about your life. Include things like what you are learning from the Word, what your plans are for the summer or how school is going this semester – anything that catches people up on what you are doing. Send it to everyone on your list.

Method

1. Schedule: Here is a possible schedule pattern of how to begin your support trail.

Week 1: Send letters to the top ten people on your list of possible supporters.

Week 2: Call the top ten people and schedule support appointments for next week. Send letters to next ten people on your list.

Week 3: Have support appointments with the top ten people. Call people from Week 2 and schedule appointments. Send support letters to the next ten people on your list.

Week 4: Call people from week 1 to find out if they have decided to join your team. Write thank you letters to them for each appointment. Have appointments with week 2 people. Call people from week 3 and schedule appointments for next week. Send support letters to the next ten people on your list.

Week 5: Keep going through the process of waves until you have full support.

2. Referrals: Ask friends for referrals to continue your support trail. This is an important part of the process, because you never run out of possible supporters on your list. For example: at the end of a support appointment, say:

"There is one other way that you could help me. Could you make a list of 5-10 people you know who might be interested in hearing about my ministry?"

3. Set Goals: Plan to make about 10 phone calls and send 10 letters a week, so that you don't get behind on your schedule.

Final Thoughts:

Raising support is one of the biggest reasons people are kept from participating in ministry. What a tragedy! The misconceptions that surround support leave a person feeling scared, insecure, and humiliated about the idea. The truth about it is that God intended His church body to be interdependent, and you will experience incredible blessing when you step out and trust in His means of provision for you! Not only will you be encouraged by the process, but those on your team will enjoy the involvement in ministry that you allow them to have. Don't let support keep you from the participating in the advance of His Kingdom!

The Ten Modules

The Traveling Team

thetravelingteam.org

> Find the greatest collection of mission resources, bible studies, articles and tools online at thetraveilngteam.org. Browse through thousands of timeless articles and updated information that will help you get started.

Mission Revolution

missionrev.org

Are you looking for speakers to help awaken your church or campus ministry? For over 15 years Mission Revolution has brought a new kind of mission conference to thousands all over the world, customized to your needs.

MissionAgency.org

missionagency.org

Are you feeling stuck and not knowing where to start? Let us match you with an opportunity in global mission. We help you work backward from God's mission to how you might fit with personal coaching and connecting from our staff who will help direct you to some of the best mission agencies in the world.

The Ten Modules

CPSIA information can be obtained
at www.ICGtesting.com
Printed in the USA
LVOW10s0326070418
572558LV00002BA/2/P